D0709488

CALGARY PUBLIC LIBRARY

SEP   2015

Praise for Gregory K. Popcak, Ph.D.

"Dr. Greg Popcak is gifted in helping individuals discover how the Church's teaching about marital love is supported by the best research in psychology and human development."
—Archbishop Joseph Naumann, Archdiocese of Kansas City, KS

"I am truly grateful for your service to the Church and for your excellent promotion and application of St. John Paul II's theology of the body. Your work is greatly needed."
—Bishop Kevin C. Rhoades, Diocese of Fort Wayne, IN

"Dr. Greg Popcak's work affirming marriage and family life . . . is well known. I am confident [the faithful] will be blessed by it."   **—Bishop David Zubik, Diocese of Pittsburgh**

"Dr. Popcak is a blessing to my diocese and to the whole Church."
—Bishop Jeffrey Monforton, Diocese of Steubenville, OH

"Dr. Greg Popcak's ministry does truly admirable work helping couples and families understand and live out the fullness of marriage and family life."
—Rev. Richard Warner, CSC, Superior General, Congregation of the Holy Cross, Rome

"Dr. Popcak is a faithful, learned, Catholic man with mountains of experience working with couples. . . . I am confident spouses who follow his advice will become better partners."
—Dr. Janet Smith, Michael J. McGivny Chair of Life Ethics, Sacred Heart Seminary, Detroit

"Dr. Popcak takes up St. John Paul II's theology of the body and lays out a whole new way of thinking about sex—God's way."
—Dr. Thomas Williams, senior research fellow, Center for Ethics and Culture, University of Notre Dame

"By combining theological insights and psychological wisdom, Dr. Popcak offers a different path to men and women looking for a way to find happiness."
—W. Bradford Wilcox, director, National Marriage Project, Univ. of Virginia

"Dr. Greg Popcak is a man after my own heart and his work is a gift to the Church."
—Christopher West, The Cor Project

"Dr. Greg Popcak articulates a practical vision of family life that is deeply faithful, extravagantly loving, and incredibly joyful."
—Damon Owens, executive director of the Theology of the Body Institute

"With a mature style that is intellectually appealing, Popcak shares his inspiring conviction that marriage can be a powerfully actualizing enterprise. . . . Like Stephen Covey and Abraham Harold Maslow, Popcak focuses on the refinement of peak performance. . . . self-improvement aficionados will find his approach a welcome and refreshing addition to the genre."

—Publishers Weekly on *The Exceptional Seven Percent: The Nine Secrets of the World's Happiest Couples*

"Popcak believes the battle against anxiety is a spiritual as well as psychological one. By relying on God's grace and applying proven techniques, no one need be driven crazy by the unavoidable stress of daily living."
—Publishers Weekly on *God Help Me! This Stress Is Driving Me Crazy!*

"Popcak brings a marriage counselor's heart and a comedian's wit to this resource on love and marriage. . . . Any couple wanting to improve their marriage will benefit from Popcak's practical, well-presented advice."
—Christian Booksellers Association Marketplace on *For Better . . . Forever!*

"This book's uniquely Catholic approach to parenting combines vigorous relational advice with careful theology and plenty of good humor."
—Publishers Weekly on *Parenting with Grace*

"This is a practical book. [Readers] will find it useful in challenging people who make life miserable for them. As a bonus, Popcak writes with a humor readers may appreciate."
—The Christian Century on *God Help Me! These People Are Driving Me Nuts!*

ALSO BY DR. GREG POPCAK

Christian Living

God Help Me, These People Are Driving Me Nuts! Making Peace with Difficult People

God Help Me, This Stress Is Driving Me Crazy!
Finding Balance Through God's Grace

The Life God Wants YOU to Have: Discovering the
Divine Plan When Human Plans Fail

Marriage

For Better . . . FOREVER! A Catholic Guide to
Lifelong Marriage (with Lisa Popcak)

The Exceptional Seven Percent: Nine Secrets of the World's Happiest Couples

Just Married: The Catholic Guide to Surviving and Thriving in
the First Five Years of Marriage (with Lisa Popcak)

Holy Sex! The Catholic Guide to Toe-Curling, Mind-Blowing, Infallible Loving

When Divorce Is Not an Option: How to Heal Your
Marriage and Nurture Lasting Love

Living a Joy-Filled Marriage—A Marriage Preparation Program

A Marriage Made for Heaven—12 Session Marriage Enrichment
Program with DVD (with Lisa Popcak)

Parenting

Parenting with Grace: The Catholic Parents' Guide to Raising
(Almost) Perfect Kids (with Lisa Popcak)

Beyond the Birds and the Bees: Raising Sexually Whole
and Holy Kids (with Lisa Popcak)

And Then Comes Baby: The Catholic Guide to Surviving and Thriving
in the First Three Years of Parenthood (with Lisa Popcak)

Broken Gods

Hope, Healing, and the
Seven Longings of the Human Heart

Gregory K. Popcak, Ph.D.

IMAGE

New York

Copyright © 2015 by Gregory K. Popcak, Ph.D.

All rights reserved.
Published in the United States by Image, an imprint
of the Crown Publishing Group, a division of
Penguin Random House LLC, New York.
www.crownpublishing.com

IMAGE is a registered trademark and the "I" colophon
is a trademark of Penguin Random House LLC.

Library of Congress Cataloging-in-Publication
data is available upon request.

ISBN 978-0-8041-4115-4
eBook ISBN 978-0-8041-4116-1

Printed in the United States of America

Jacket design by Gabe Levine
Jacket photograph: LeksusTuss/Shutterstock

10 9 8 7 6 5 4 3 2 1

First Edition

The only-begotten Son of God, wanting to make us sharers in his divinity, assumed our nature, so that he, made man, might make men gods.

—St. Thomas Aquinas

Contents

Chapter One

More Than You Can Imagine

Imagine that you were to wake up tomorrow to discover that, by some miracle, you had become a god overnight. Not *the* God—omnipresent, all-knowing, all-powerful—but *a* god in the classic sense. That is to say, you wake to find that you are perfect, immortal, utterly confident in *who* you are, *where* you are going in life, and *how* you are going to get there. It might seem ridiculous to consider at first, but allow yourself to imagine this truly miraculous transformation. What would it be like to live without fear? How would it feel to be completely at peace with yourself and the people in your life? Imagine what it would be like to be able to resolve—once and for all—the tension that currently exists between all your competing feelings, impulses, desires, and demands. What would change in your life as a result of your having become that sort of divinely actualized person?

Perhaps a better question would be "What wouldn't change?"

What Does God See When He Looks at You?

What you've just imagined is exactly the destiny God has in store for you. The truth is, God really and truly intends to make you a god—a being who is perfect, whole, healed, and, yes, even immortal. "So whoever is in Christ is a new creation: the old things have passed away; behold, new things have come" (2 Cor 5:17). Christians often talk about "being saved," but more than being saved *from* something (i.e., sin) the truth is, we are saved *for* something—to become divine!

The idea seems crazy, maybe even blasphemous, but that's only because we are used to seeing ourselves as the world sees us—broken, struggling, failing, and frustrated. But when God looks at you, an eternal and boundless love wells up inside him and he sees past every doubt, every fear, everything you think is shameful or broken about you. When God looks at you, he sees something more beautiful, remarkable, and amazing than you could ever even wrap your head around. In the words of St. John Paul the Great, *"We are not the sum of our weaknesses and failures; we are the sum of the Father's love for us and our real capacity to become the image of his Son"* (Pope John Paul II, 2002).

When God looks at you, he sees within you the fulfillment of every hope, every dream, every desire, and every potentiality. In short, when God looks at you, *he sees a god.*

I am not spinning some beautiful illusion. The *doctrine* that humans are destined, through Christ, to become gods is a lost treasure that is at the very heart of Christianity. Hidden in plain sight, it is a truth that can transform every part of your spiritual, emotional, and relational life if you know how to claim it.

Become Everything You Are Meant to Be

In the following pages, not only will you discover the incredible vision God has for your life; you will also come to see that the parts of yourself you like the least, the temptations that tear you apart, the longings you seem never to be able to satisfy, the desires you try to repress, can, through God's grace, reveal the path to the new creation God wants to make of you. Most important, you will discover, step-by-step, how to transform the weakest, most broken, and even shameful parts of yourself into the engine of your perfection.

First, we'll explore the shocking truth about *divinization,* the ancient and surprisingly orthodox Christian assertion that God truly intends to make you a god and what that means, practically speaking, for your life today. Next, I will reveal how your desires, even your darkest and most troublesome passions, expose the engine God intends to use to work this amazing transformation in your life. Finally, I will present a step-by-step plan for cooperating more effectively with the miracle God wants to work in you so that you might experience the deep joy that comes from both satisfying the *seven divine longings* of your heart and fulfilling your destiny to become the god you were meant, by God, to be.

"You Are Gods!"

Theologians use terms such as "deification," "divine filiation," "theosis," and, as I mentioned above, "divinization" to refer to God's incredible plan to make those who love him into gods. Although these words can be a mouthful, each term is just another way of saying you are destined for a greatness beyond your wildest imaginings! Whatever crazy dreams you have for your life, God has you beat—hands down. By means of his epic and eternal love for you, God intends to make you a god—perfect, whole, healed, fearless, living abundantly in this life and reigning forever by his side in the next.

The remarkable truth that God became a human being so that human beings might become gods is revealed in Scripture. The Second Letter of Peter (1:4) says that through Christ's saving work we become "partakers of the divine nature." Likewise, it was Jesus who said, "Be perfect, as your heavenly Father is perfect" (Mt 5:48). When we read that passage today, we often think it means, "Jesus wants us to be really, really good," but Christianity has always taught that this verse means much more. Jesus told us so when he reminded the Pharisees, "Is it not written in your law, 'I have said, "You are gods"'?" (Jn 10:34, in which Christ quotes Ps 82:6). C. S. Lewis notes the miraculous significance of this passage when he writes in *Mere Christianity*,

> "Be ye perfect" is not idealistic gas. Nor is it a command to do the impossible. He is going to make us into creatures that can obey that command. He said (in the Bible) that we were "gods" and He is going to make good His words. If we let Him . . . He will make the feeblest and filthiest of us into a god or goddess, dazzling, radiant, immortal creatures, pulsating all through with such energy and joy and wisdom and love as we cannot now imagine, a bright stainless mirror which reflects back to Him perfectly (Lewis, 1952).

Early Christian leaders and saints wrote widely on the topic of divinization. The authors of the *Catechism of the Catholic Church* gathered some of their more prominent reflections on this concept in their response to the question "Why did God become man?"

The Word became flesh to make us *"partakers of the divine nature"* (2 Pt 1:4): "For this is why the Word became man, and the Son of God became the Son of man: so that man, by entering into communion with the Word and thus receiving divine sonship, might become a son of God" (St. Irenaeus). "For the Son of God became man so that we might become God" (St. Athanasius). "The only-begotten Son of God, wanting to make us sharers in his divinity, assumed our nature, so that he, made man, might make men gods" (St. Thomas Aquinas) (*CCC,* no. 460).

The *Catechism* isn't cherry-picking random quotes from fringe figures. These sayings come from some of the greatest minds in the history of Christendom, all of whom are universally respected by Catholics, Orthodox, and Protestants alike for their scholarship and their sanctity. Moreover, these few quotes cited by the *Catechism* are only a small sample of a much wider pool of similar quotes dating back to the earliest days of Christianity. For instance,

[In the beginning, humans] were made like God, free from suffering and death, provided that they kept His commandments, and were deemed deserving of the name of His sons, and yet they, becoming like Adam and Eve, work out death for themselves; let the interpretation of the Psalm be held just as you wish, yet thereby it is demonstrated that all men are deemed worthy of becoming "gods," and of having power to become sons of the Highest.

—*St. Justin Martyr, c. AD 100–165*
(Dialogue with Trypho, *chapter 124*)

[H]e who listens to the Lord, and follows the prophecy given by Him, will be formed perfectly in the likeness of the teacher—made a god going about in flesh.

—*St. Clement of Alexandria, c. AD 150–215*
(The Stromata, *7.16 (book 7, chapter 16)*)

From the Holy Spirit is the likeness of God, and the highest thing to be desired, to become God.

—*St. Basil the Great, c. AD 330–379 (*De Spiritu Sanctu*)*

If we have been made sons of God, we have also been made gods.

—*St. Augustine, c. AD 354–430 (*Exposition on Psalm 50*)*

The idea that we are destined to become gods through God's love and grace was supported by the Protestant reformers as well. John Calvin wrote, "The end of the gospel is, to render us eventually conformable to God, and, if we may so speak, to deify us" (Wedgeworth, 2011).

Martin Luther also took up the theme of deification when he preached, "God pours out Christ His dear Son over us and pours Himself into us and draws us into Himself, so that He becomes completely humanified (*vemzenschet*) and we become completely deified (*gantz und gar vergottet,* 'Godded-through') and everything is altogether one thing, God, Christ, and you" (Marquardt, 2000).

Perhaps the most shocking thing about this promise of God to make us gods is that it generated virtually no controversy within the early Christian communities. This is incredibly odd because the first few centuries of Christianity were rocked by epic arguments even about the nature of

Christ. Despite this, there is no record of any first-century Christian seeming the slightest bit put out by the idea that human beings are destined to become divine through the saving work of Jesus Christ. In the words of theologian Juan Gonzalez Arintero, "So common were these ideas concerning deification that not even the heretics of the first centuries dared to deny them" (1979). Indeed, Arintero goes on to say, "This deification, so well known to the Fathers but unfortunately forgotten today, *is the primary purpose of the Christian life.*"

As you can see, divinization is a foundational teaching of mainline Christianity, but it is a lost treasure. Of course, there is only One True God. But we are made in his image and likeness and, because of the saving work of Jesus Christ, we have been gathered up into the life of God, and become partakers in that divinity.

Why Should We Care?

But so what? What's all this to us? Sure, it's a provocative idea, but what difference does it really make? It would be easy to write off divinization as just some moldy theological concept. But it is so much more. Though we are often tempted to feel that our lives and hopes and dreams are burning down around us, deification is the blueprint that allows us to rebuild our lives from the ashes and become everything God intended us to be from the beginning. It is the treasure map that helps us to rediscover just how truly wonderfully and fearfully we have been made (Ps 139:14). Understanding deification enables us to finally stop running *from* our sins and instead begin running *toward* divinity. It enables us to become not only our best selves, but so much more besides. When we embrace the idea that God wishes to make us gods, we are set free from fear and encounter within our hearts the peace this world cannot give (Jn 14:27). Along the way we become empowered to resolve all the conflicts that fill our days with exhausting, petty dramas and instead experience radical, harmonious union with both God and the people who share our lives (Jn 17:21). Most important, God's plan for our divinization enables us to stop the constant emptiness and aching of our hearts and sets us on a path of abundance and the authentic fulfillment of all of our earthly and heavenly desires (Jn 10:10).

In addition, the idea of divinization helps place in proper context the central and critical Christian belief that we are broken and in need of salvation. Prominent atheist blogger Neil Carter illustrates the importance of this belief in his article "We Are Not Broken," where he writes of his frustration in finding common language with even progressive Christians who agree with him on so many social issues.

But then I suggest that human beings *aren't broken*— they aren't sinful or lacking something essential to their wholeness—that they just are what they are and they're not "supposed to be" something else and then the conversation changes. I've just touched on something bedrock for them, immovable. . . . This belief—that the human condition is fundamentally flawed—is so central and necessary to their way of thinking. . . . *If you take away human inadequacy, you take away the basis for the Christian faith.* If you don't believe me, then try it sometime. Try to suggest that we are fine the way we are. Not perfect, mind you. Not flawless or infallible. But not fundamentally messed up, either—not broken, not wounded, not inadequate— and watch what happens next. They won't have it. *You can't take this away from them* (Carter, 2014).

Carter gets at what many Christians themselves struggle to understand and certainly can't articulate to others. Atheists like to think they are being optimistic about human nature— that it is Christians who are down on humanity. But atheists like Carter are lost in pessimism without even knowing it. From the very beginning, Christianity taught that humans were not meant to be merely human. We are, in fact, *broken gods*. Because of the reality of sin, humanity has lost its *divinity,* and it is exactly this "life more abundant" (Jn 10:10) that Jesus Christ came to restore. You, and I, and Neil Carter might want to believe that we are fine just the way we are, but we are not gods—we are not perfect and immortal—not yet, anyway, but by God's grace that is exactly what we are meant to become!

Divinity or Narcissism?

As amazing as this divine promise to transform us into gods is, it's critical to recognize that we neither can claim this divinity for ourselves nor can we generate it on our own. Divinization is a gift that we receive as we run with abandon into the loving arms of the God who made us and who longs to complete his miraculous work in us. Only by acknowledging this truth can we avoid confusing God's promise of divinization with simple New Age self-aggrandizement.

Building on this, there are three points that theologian Peter Kreeft says separate the Christian view of divinization from the New Age pretense of a quasi-divine humanity: *piety, objective morality,* and *worship* (1988).

Piety compels the Christian to proclaim that there is something greater than we are. For the most part, New Agers and neopagans believe that humans are divine on our own merits (Zeller, 2014). But the Christian view of divinization recognizes that we do not claim divinity as an essential dimension of humanity. "If you, Lord, keep account of sins, who could stand?" (Ps 130:3). Christians recognize that especially in light of the Fall, humanity is deserving of anything but deification. It is only through Jesus Christ, our Savior, that we are able to achieve the greatest of heights, daring to look God in the eye and see him, not as our Master, but as our "friend" (Jn 15:15) with whom we can rightfully expect to enter into a total union through his infinite, divine mercy.

Second, Christians acknowledge an *objective morality.* New Agers believe in many moralities and a multiplicity of truths. The moral reasoning of the modern neopagan represents a polytheism of "many gods, many goods, many moralities" (Kreeft, 1988). In the New Age model of human divinity (or divine humanity), *I* am the author of my own truth, not God. It is my self-anointed right to pretend that I am capable of making reality whatever I say it is simply by closing my eyes and wishing on myself.

By contrast, the Christian acknowledges that there is a natural, objective order to the world, which was ordained by God, and to which his children are obliged to adhere, not out of a sense of slavish devotion to alien rules, but so that we might fulfill our incredible destiny to become gods through God's grace. Our ability to accomplish this awesome task depends in large part on our active participation in this divinely created moral order because "nothing unclean can enter the Kingdom of Heaven" (Rv 21:27).

The third point that distinguishes the Christian notion of deification from the New Age notion is that the modern neo-pagan fails to *worship* anyone, ultimately, besides himself. He takes his de facto divinity for granted and demands that you acknowledge it too despite the fact that there is no evidence of godliness in his person or his behavior. He believes he can do what he will—even if it hurts you—because he is divine, the master of his own destiny, and responsible only to his own personal sense of self-fulfillment.

In contrast, the Christian approaches the notion that he is destined to become a god with a sense of wonder, awe, amazement, gratitude, and not a little bit of fear born of the recognition that there are serious forces at play within this promise. And yet, even that understandable fear is cast out by the perfect love (see 1 Jn 4:18) that flows from the heart of the God who calls to us, runs to meet us on the road, and wraps his finest cloak—his divinity—around us (see Lk 15:22).

The Christian call for each person to participate in God's plan to make men gods is not an exercise in narcissism or wish fulfillment. It does not serve as a get-out-of-morality-free card. It is an invitation, rooted in the love of our heavenly Father, for each one of us and extended to all of humanity through the saving work of Jesus Christ. Furthermore, it is an invitation God has been extending to humanity since the beginning of time.

Once upon a Time . . .

At the dawn of creation, God intended great things for us, but our first parents' tragic downfall in the Garden of Eden caused a fundamental disconnect between us and God that resulted in a profound warping of our humanity. Though we were made in God's image, the Fall caused humankind to take our eyes off God's face, preventing us from seeing our destiny reflected in God's eyes. By turning away from God, our first parents shattered the internal mirror that enabled them to reflect the image of God and achieve the fullness of their perfected nature. This first catastrophic choice teaches us that when we deny God, we ultimately deny and then destroy ourselves.

Through Jesus's incarnation, God began the process of healing our essential brokenness, our fallen humanity, from the inside out. By becoming flesh, God inserted an ember of his divinity into the heart of creation. With this divine spark growing within us, God began to melt and untwist our hearts of iron, refining us into the pure gold he made us to be.

The incarnation, then, is the opening paragraph of the invitation God sends to all of humankind announcing his intention to transform us into gods. But though the incarnation redeems our basic humanity, the incarnation cannot save individual people unless they respond to it and cooperate in the process of transformation. Invitations require an RSVP, so God gives us a way to answer his call. Our baptism represents the second paragraph of God's invitation and the next step in our transformation. Baptism is our personal "yes" to the intimate movement of God in our lives. It imprints God's family seal on our hearts (Sg 8:6) and commits us to the process of allowing God's grace to transform us into the gods we are meant to be (Jn 3:5). In the third paragraph of the invitation, God prepares a feast, the Eucharist, and invites us to *become* his flesh and blood by *consuming* his real flesh and blood (Jn 6:55), the food that sustains us on our divine journey and heals the radical disconnect between us, God, and the world.

You Are More Than Meets the Eye

Through these gifts, God sets in motion powerful forces that make us not only whole, but also something more than we could ever hope to become through our own meager efforts. Because of God's great gifts, we are no longer defined by our weakness. We are defined by the abundant love our heavenly Father has for us and the destiny that Christ Jesus's passion, death, and resurrection makes possible. In the words of St. John XXIII, "Consult not your fears but your hopes and your dreams. Think not about your frustrations, but about your unfulfilled potential. Concern yourself not with what you tried and failed in, but with what is still possible" (Meconi, 2014).

Most of us can't even begin to realize what our potential—indeed, our destiny—truly is. But St. John XXIII reminds us that for Christians *"what is still possible"* is nothing less than fulfilling the divine plan that *we, ourselves, are to become divine.*

Again and again, God calls out to us, and whether we realize it or not, a part of our deepest self has been programmed to reach back to God. Like a homing beacon pinging out in the darkness, this part of us relentlessly reminds us that we are not yet where we belong and we must hurry to find our way back home again. As Augustine said, "Our hearts are restless until they find their rest in you, God." So what is this homing beacon? Nothing less than the sum of our desires fiercely fighting to break free of the chains that frustrate their desperate longing for ultimate fulfillment.

The Inner Ache

We all ache for "more." We want more. We want to have more. We want to *be* more. But many of us believe that we are simply being selfish when we indulge these fantasies of abundance. Of course, there are any number of people who, at any moment, would be more than happy to tell you that thinking you were meant for more is an exercise in narcissistic self-delusion.

It is true that we often attempt to satisfy this ache in ways that will never fill us up. But this doesn't alter the fact that our universal longings point to *something* beyond ourselves. Too often our response is to shut down our desires or give in to those people in our lives who try to shout them down.

There is another option. We can learn to listen to what that ache for more is really saying to us about both our destiny and the means of fulfilling it. There is nothing wrong with the desire for more. In fact, God promises to fulfill that ache: "Find your delight in the Lord who will give you your heart's desire" (Ps 37:4). The insatiable ache in our hearts—misguided though it can be—is incredibly important. It exists to remind us that we were destined by God *to be gods* and to motivate us to commit to live a life that makes God's stunningly amazing plans for us possible. Each and every one of our desires—including our earthly desires and even our sinful desires—exists to point the way back home to God. Unfortunately, many of the things we do—whether we are trying to fulfill our destiny or simply to quench that more immediate, burning hunger—end up breaking us. Our divine homing beacon is in need of repair. Its tone still sounds and echoes in the ground of our being, but it does not always point us in a true direction. Out of frustration, many people try to ignore the constant pinging of this beacon hidden at the core of their desires. Others simply go wherever the beacon superficially points them, never questioning the direction they are heading in until they become more and more lost.

Despite these challenges, we can still find our way back to God and back to our destiny in God. We are meant to be gods, but because of our fallen humanity, we are, for now, *broken gods* in need of deeper healing—a healing that God makes possible through his divine gifts and our own efforts to stop living in fear of our deepest desires, the seven divine longings of every human heart. When we turn our longings over to him, he sets us on the path to becoming the gods we were created to be—whole and healed, peaceful and perfect, faithful, fearless, and *fulfilled*.

Chapter Two

The Seven Divine Longings of the Human Heart

Do not be afraid!

—*Matthew 14:27*

Embrace the divine filiation which
constitutes the essence of the Good News.

—*St. John Paul the Great,*

Crossing the Threshold of Hope

We spend a great deal of our lives consumed by fears of one kind or another. Perhaps the greatest fears are those fears that alienate us from ourselves.

What if there were a way to stop being afraid of your desires? In this chapter, you will discover how even your most neurotic and destructive desires can be transformed into engines of divine actualization that can propel you down the path toward both a more joyful life in the present and the fulfillment of your ultimate destiny, becoming the god that God himself created you to be.

Love and the Reorientation of Desire

Falling in love with my wife was a transformational experience for me. Suddenly, everything was about her. Love has a way of radically reorienting us away from ourselves and toward one another. We find ourselves by losing ourselves.

In a similar way, when we make an authentic response to God's invitation to become gods, something amazing happens. Suddenly everything is about him. Our hopes, our dreams, our relationships, *our desires* become reoriented. They don't go away, but they take on a new significance. They point not to our desires as an end in themselves, but to new ways we might come to know God better and draw closer to him. Directly or indirectly, our desires become entirely about him.

The Three Attitudes Toward Desire

We desire a lot of things: wealth, status, power, sex, security, affirmation, and health are just a few of the longings almost every person aches to fulfill. Sadly, we often have a complicated relationship with our desires. In his book *Fill These Hearts* (2012), Christopher West notes that, in the face of their desires, people tend to become either *addicts, stoics,* or *mystics.*

The Addict

Those who adopt the addict mind-set tend to unquestioningly surrender to their desires, whatever they may be. Although the term "addict" could involve actual addictions, West uses the term more metaphorically. The addict tends to assume that his or her devotion to sex, food, money, status, esteem, emotional extremes, drugs, alcohol, and the like is a good thing and is largely beyond his or her ability to control it. Many of us adopt the posture of the addict in some area of our lives when we find our passions or desires consuming us and complicating our lives in some way.

Addicts tend to think that the *strength* of their desires is the problem. But, properly understood and gracefully ordered, strong desires can actually fuel our divinization! The real problem is that instead of seeing that desire points to something greater, the addict makes an idol out of desire itself (Pargament, 2011). The pursuit of these idols—whether chemical addictions, habitual obsessions, or codependent relationships—can imitate the *feeling* of transcendence we have when we experience an authentically sacred moment, but, ultimately, these compulsions cause disintegration and conflict instead of the integration and peace that come from the real thing (Pargament, 2011). The problem with these common idols is not that they are sources of pleasure, but that ultimately *they are not pleasurable enough.*

God created us so that every desire we have will ultimately point to our essential longing for deep intimacy with him. Unfortunately, instead of reaching for the encounter with the sacred hidden on just the other side of our earthly desires, addicts settle for the pleasure of the moment. Ironically, the more we settle, the more unsettled we feel. The result is an even more obsessive relationship with the idol. We return again and again to the dry well hoping that *this time* our thirst will be quenched. In the words of culture commentator and author Mark Shea, "You can never get enough of what you don't really want" (2001).

Question for reflection: In the face of what desires do you tend to adopt the attitude of the addict?

The Stoic

By contrast, stoics live in fear and/or denial of their desires. Whether they have been burned by their own passions or damaged by someone else's attempt to use them as an object of desire, stoics try to deny that they have any real desires, and as a consequence they tend to become bitter and angry. They are the "querulous, and disillusioned pessimists, [the] 'sourpusses'" that Pope Francis decried in *Evangelium Gaudii* [The joy of the gospel] (2013).

Each of us can name times when we weren't truthful about our needs, or when our attempts to repress our desires made us resentful. But when this stance becomes a way of life, stoicism can be the source of tremendous pain. Stoics often suffer from what psychologists call *internal sacred conflicts* (Pargament, 2011). In other words, when two spiritual goods appear to clash (for instance, the desire for intimacy vs. the desire for freedom, or the desire for sexual fulfillment vs. the desire to be faithful), stoics will try to repress or even destroy the desire they consider more troublesome instead of learning to fulfill both desires in a healthy way. Unfortunately, repressed desires always fight back with a vengeance. The more stoical we are about our desires, the more likely it is that we will condemn ourselves to a perpetual cycle of repressive denial followed by secret self-indulgence, leading, ultimately, to disintegration of the self.

Question for reflection: When are you more likely to play the stoic in the face of your desires?

Neither the addict's nor the stoic's attitude toward desire is consistent with the call to become gods through God's grace. Divinization is about both the ultimate integration of the person and the total restoration of our relationship with God, but the postures the addict and stoic adopt toward desire lead to dis-integration of the person and alienation from an authentic experience of God. Fortunately, there is a third way, the way of the mystic.

The Mystic

Most people think of a mystic as someone who sits on a mountaintop, cut off from humanity and devoting all of his time to thinking deep thoughts. In truth, every Christian is called to be a mystic. In the Christian tradition, a mystic is simply someone who experiences God behind and within each moment, who sees that God is reaching out to us through even the most mundane and even the most profane human experiences. *The mystic sees his or her desires as a door to heaven* and understands that by connecting with the deeper realities to which our desires point, we can find true fulfillment.

"I love food," Aaron says. "I enjoy trying new things, going to new restaurants, cooking new recipes, but I never really thought of it as anything more than that, until this past year when I had kind of an epiphany.

"Enjoying eating as I do, I always saw fasting as this punitive thing. But this past Lent, I was sitting in my car after Mass, just sort of lost in thought. As I sat there, I just had this question come to mind, 'What are you hungry for?' At first, my mind started wandering to the places I like to go for brunch after

Mass with my friends, but I just felt like God was nudging me to go a little deeper. I just kept hearing, 'What are you hungry for?' and I thought, 'You, Lord. I'm hungry for you. Fill me up.' I just sat there like that for . . . I don't know, a few seconds, maybe a minute. It wasn't a long time, but it felt eternal or something. I remember tearing up. I wasn't sad. I just felt . . . open. I can't say I've ever really felt anything quite like it before. The more I reflected on that time, I realized that this was the whole point of fasting. It wasn't that food was bad, or God was saying that I should probably lose a few, or that good meals were somehow sinful. Fasting was an opportunity to remind myself of my hunger for God. That, as much as I enjoy my favorite brunch place, the only thing that can really satisfy my deepest hungers is God. I haven't been quite the same since. Strangely, I think I enjoy food even more now. I still love going out to eat and trying new recipes, but eating has taken on a whole new dimension for me. It's not just pleasurable, it has become more spiritual. Does that make sense? I open a menu and remember that God wants to, like the Psalm says, 'spread a table before me,' a table of all of his blessings and grace, and I just feel this urge to take a quiet moment to thank God for his blessings and tell him that I love him. And in those times when I'm fasting or dieting (because, you know, I love to eat), the hunger I feel isn't just something to suffer through. It reminds me that as much as God wants to satisfy all my longings and desires, the thing he most wants to give me is himself. I just have to open my heart to ask him to 'fill me up.' Eating, not eating, it all just seems more satisfying. It all just means . . . more."

Aaron hasn't been the same since his encounter with God in his car after Mass because none of us is quite the same when we are falling in love. I began this section on desire by sharing how falling in love with my wife made me want to make everything about her. Falling in love with God involves a similar process. God doesn't want to take away our desires for lesser things; he just wants to show us how to satisfy those desires in truly fulfilling ways, and he wants to remind us that the thing we were made to desire most is him.

Divinization and the Evolution of Desire

Christian mystics over the centuries have discovered that divinization refines our desires through three distinct stages or "ways." First, in the *purgative way* we experience a rehabilitation of desire as God shows us how to satisfy our earthly desires in healthy ways. Next, in the *illuminative way* we experience the enlightenment of desire as we discover that God has been reaching out to us through our longings and wants to reveal himself to us through them. Finally, in the *unitive way* we experience the unification of our desires with the very heart of God. In each stage, both our flawed desires and the misguided ways we try to satisfy them undergo a transformation as we prepare to achieve the ultimate fulfillment of our divine destiny. Through this process, we learn that God is not the enemy of our desires; rather he seeks to satisfy our desires to a degree that we didn't know was possible. He longs to meet the deepest needs of our heart—even needs beyond our awareness.

But where do we start? Having accepted the invitation to theosis that God extends to us, how do we begin to walk this incredible path toward becoming the gods we were meant to be?

Seven Deadly Sins

We make a ladder for ourselves of our vices, if we trample those same vices underfoot.

—*St. Augustine (Sermon III.* De Ascensione*)*

Remarkably, our journey toward deification takes wing when we allow God's perfect love to cast out the fear we experience in the face of our darkest desires, the *seven deadly sins:* pride, lust, envy, greed, gluttony, wrath, and sloth. That rogues' gallery of imperfections. The seven deadly sins represent the longings we all hate to love and love to hate, longings that consume all too much of our time, effort, and energy.

Hidden Within Sin: A Hint of Hope?

People often despair over their endless struggles against their fallen nature. But what if I told you that, rather than a cause for despair, the very existence of the seven deadly sins is a sign of hope? The seven deadly sins actually point toward the seven divine longings of every human heart. Longings that God not only approves of but intends to satisfy abundantly!

Classically, sin is understood as "a privation of the good." To put it another way, sin is settling for less than what God wants to give you. For instance, God wants us to experience earthly pleasures in a way that leads us to greater health and stronger relationships and points us toward fulfilling our destiny in him. Instead, we tend to settle for particular types of experiences of earthly pleasure that are destructive to our health and well-being, that undermine our relationships, and that point us toward nothing except emptiness. Sin does not make us "bad people." It makes us broken people—really, broken gods, because divinization is our destiny. Sin steals this destiny from us and turns us into people who feel powerless and isolated, people who are filled with self-pity and consumed by the pursuit of self-indulgence because they want to make all the pain go away.

By contrast, because he loves us, God wants us to desire what is good for us, and through our deepest longings he wants us to be healed. So he gives us the grace to fulfill all our desires—even the earthly ones—in a dynamic way that satisfies body, mind, and spirit!

Give Me a Drink

Consider the story of the Samaritan woman's encounter with Jesus at the well. Jesus asks her for a drink, and after a brief exchange he reveals that he has much more in mind for her.

> Jesus answered and said to her, "Everyone who drinks this water will be thirsty again; but whoever drinks the water I shall give will never thirst; the water I shall give will become in him a spring of water welling up to eternal life." The woman said to him, "Sir, give me this water, so that I may not be thirsty or have to keep coming here to draw water" (Jn 4:13-15).

As the story unfolds, we discover that the woman at the well has had five husbands and is now living with a paramour. Clearly, this is a woman who is looking for something more and struggling to find it. It would be easy to condemn her, but that would mean ignoring something important: *the strength of her desires is actually a great resource.* Unlike many who give up, believing that their longings can never be satisfied, she continues to look for something that can fill her. Like that Samaritan woman of long ago, each of us stands before Christ thirsting, but we're uncertain about what we are thirsty for. We seek fulfillment in the pursuit of pleasure as an end in itself, but no pleasure will ever satisfy us. We can discover the living water that quenches our thirst only when we turn to Christ, who shows us that when our desires for earthly things are united with his grace, they can serve as vehicles that propel us toward true fulfillment and our ultimate destiny.

Deadly Sins Versus Divine Longings

And so, as I asserted at the beginning of this section, the seven deadly sins are actually a sign of hope because, despite their best attempt to obscure them, their very presence reveals the existence of the *seven divine longings of the human heart,* namely, our deep, hidden, but inescapable yearnings for *abundance, dignity, justice, peace, trust, well-being,* and *communion,* respectively. These seven divine longings have such tremendous potential to propel us toward divinization that Satan works hard to keep them hidden where we are least likely to look, behind the parts of ourselves we hate the most.

Virtue: Not Enough?

Over the centuries, the church has presented the *seven heavenly virtues* as the classic antidote to the seven deadly sins. For instance, pride is meant to be healed through *humility*, envy by *kindness*, wrath by *patience*, sloth through *diligence*, greed through *generosity*, gluttony through *temperance*, and lust by *chastity*. These ancient spiritual antidotes have been reaffirmed over centuries of practice and reflection. Yet there are three common problems that occur when people try to counter the deadly sins with the heavenly virtues.

First, people often have a poor understanding of what these virtues require. For example, discovering that patience is the antidote to wrath, many believe that they should feel guilty if they experience even the slightest irritation with someone who has hurt them terribly. Similarly, knowing that humility is the antidote to pride, many believe that they should never speak or think well of themselves or rejoice in their talents or accomplishments. Neither of these ideas is true. Despite our best intentions, if we don't understand what the heavenly virtues really ask of us, our attempts to avoid one serious error can bring on a different but equally serious problem.

Second, when people learn that the seven heavenly virtues are the antidotes to the seven deadly sins, they tend to think that we have to practice the seven heavenly virtues in order to "be good." This idea misses the point entirely. Heaven is not so much for the good as it is for the godly. Our divinization is driven by the *strength of our relationship with God,* not by the "goodness" we have achieved by our own efforts. Goodness may be one of the visible signs of that relationship (see Jas 2:17), but not always. We can be good for all the wrong reasons. Some people are good because they are afraid they won't be liked if they don't toe the line. Others are good because they want to get something out of you. For the Christian, goodness is not a goal in and of itself. It is the *fruit* of an authentic and vital relationship with Christ. There is a reason that *love, joy, peace, patience, kindness, generosity, faithfulness, gentleness,* and *self-control* are identified as the *fruits* of the spirit and not the *roots* of the spirit. The root, or basis, of these virtues is our relationship with Christ. Pursued on their own without this relationship solidly in place, even the greatest virtues become "a noisy gong or a clanging symbol" (1 Cor 13:1).

Third, for many people "being good," per se, is rarely a very powerful motivator. Of course, we would very much like to be good and for others to think we're good. We just seem to consistently want goodness less than we want whatever pleasure is dangled in front of us at the moment. As Oscar Wilde famously put it, "I can resist everything but temptation." The more many of us try to fight directly against our sins, the more we seem to get trapped in them.

The Seven Divine Longings: The Path to Freedom and Fulfillment

Discovering the seven divine longings of the human heart gives us a way out of the "trying and failing to be good" trap. Jesus tells us that his yoke is easy and his burden is light (Mt 11:30), but so many of us experience the exact opposite in our lives. Despite any appearances to the contrary, Jesus wasn't lying. The burden he asks us to carry *is* light. We are simply carrying the load in a manner that is breaking our backs and ruining our spiritual center of balance.

The heavenly virtues are not so much a weapon against

sin as they are a means of making sin obsolete by satisfying our divine longings. In fact, the more energy we put into identifying and meeting our divine longings by practicing the heavenly virtues, the less we feel the need to sin. When we stop fighting against our brokenness and instead simply seek to heal that brokenness by fulfilling the God-given longings hidden behind our sins, we stop working against ourselves and start working toward both our present fulfillment and our ultimate destiny to become gods through God's grace.

Let's take a closer look at how the seven deadly sins, the seven divine longings, and the seven heavenly virtues relate to one another.

Pride

Pride represents a distortion of the divine longing for *abundance,* the longing each person has to live a full, meaningful, and rewarding life. This longing for abundance is an innate gift from God. Jesus tells us that we were created to live life more abundantly and that he came to show us how (see Jn 10:10). We can learn to experience this longing for abundance as a gift from God, as something that God has given us to facilitate our divinization, something that reminds us that true fulfillment can be attained only when our restless hearts rest in God.

Pride distorts this longing for abundance by making me believe that I, and only I, have the ability to determine what living a full, meaningful, and rewarding life means. Pride tells me that attending to anyone but myself will diminish my happiness and fulfillment. Beyond this, pride tells me that I must not use my gifts in a way that serves others. To live my version of an abundant life, pride tells me I must use whatever advantage I have to set myself apart from everyone else.

Despite the lies pride tries to sell us, our longing for abundance can be satisfied only by practicing the heavenly virtue of *humility,* which has nothing to do with running ourselves down, degrading ourselves, or denying our talents or abilities. Instead, cultivating humility enables us to make peace with the fact that we need to cooperate with God and others if we want to live in abundance. Humility enables us learn from God's instruction and other people's experience. Further, humility empowers us to use the advantages we've been given to work for the good of those around us, strengthening our relationships and enabling us to work together to achieve our fullest potential.

Envy

Envy is a distortion of the divine longing for *dignity,* the desire to have our worth as persons acknowledged and celebrated. We all want to know that we are worth something, that we are valuable and that we have innate dignity. In fact, as our examination of our call to divinization shows, God longs to bestow upon us a dignity beyond anything we could imagine! In this life, the divine longing for dignity helps us realize that we are truly God's gift to the world (in the healthiest sense of that phrase)! Further, it facilitates our divinization by challenging us to become more effective instruments of God's love and care.

Envy distorts our longing for dignity by telling us that we have no worth or value unless we have everything that everyone else around us has, and that we can accomplish everything that everyone else can achieve. When we give in to envy, we see every relationship as a competition in which either we come out on top or we are the loser.

The divine longing for dignity can be truly satisfied only if we practice the heavenly virtue of *kindness.* When we practice grace-inspired kindness with others, we encourage them to bloom in our presence. Kindness enables us to discover our dignity by enabling us to become the means through which others encounter theirs.

Wrath

Wrath is a distortion of the divine longing for *justice*. In this life, the divine longing for justice prompts us to respond to offenses effectively and to restore right order. Our longing for justice is a heavenly gift. Jesus says, "Blessed are those who hunger and thirst for righteousness" (Mt 5:6). The divine longing for justice facilitates our divinization by calling us out of ourselves and reminding us to care for those around us.

Wrath distorts our divine longing for justice by compelling us to seek selfish "solutions" to our problems that hurt others as much as or as deeply as they have hurt us. Wrath perpetuates and magnifies injustice by convincing us that revenge—even petty revenge—is the best way to right wrongs.

The divine longing for justice can be satisfied only when we practice the heavenly virtue of *patience*. Contrary to popular opinion, being patient does not mean that we tolerate offenses without ever saying anything. Rather, when we cultivate patience, we demonstrate a willingness to let our good efforts to resolve injustices mature instead of trying to force hasty, half-baked "solutions" that hurt others and serve only to make things worse.

Sloth

Sloth is a distortion of the divine longing for *peace*. In this life, the divine longing for peace motivates us to live a more harmonious life. Our desire for peace is an innate call from God. In his Sermon on the Mount, Jesus says those who seek true peace will be called "blessed" (Mt 5:9). In seeking peace, we are facilitating our divinization because in the process we become more attuned to God's will. Sloth perverts our divine longing for peace because under its influence we believe that the best way to achieve peace is to close our eyes to the problems around us, keep our heads down, and avoid any potential conflict—even conflict that involves working for justice, our good, and the good of those around us.

The divine longing for peace can be satisfied only by practicing the heavenly virtue of *diligence*. In the Lord's Prayer, we say, "Thy will be done." When we're diligent we facilitate God's will no matter what the cost or how long it takes us on the only path to true peace in our lives. Diligence (aka *fortitude*) represents our commitment to cooperate with God's grace so that his will might be done in the world—or at least in our little corner of it. By diligently discerning and then courageously pursuing God's will in our lives and relationships, we can begin to assuage the ache in our hearts that is the divine longing for peace.

Greed

Greed is a distortion of the divine longing for *trust,* the desire to feel certain that both we and what we have are enough to face the challenges life hurls at us. In this life, the divine longing for trust propels us to overcome our fears. Beyond this, Scripture tells us that our divinization depends on our capacity for trust: "To those who trust in his name he has given the privilege of being children of God" (Jn 1:12).

Greed distorts this call to trust because it leads us to give in to our fears and tells us that the only security we can count on is what we can accumulate for ourselves. We know that everything can be taken away from us in one fell swoop. One turn of bad fortune. One bout of serious illness. One bad storm. One bad day and all of our security can evaporate. Our greed tells us that the only way to gain any sense of security is by stocking up more, gathering more, achieving more. Greed makes us believe that only if we can buy enough land, sow enough seed, and harvest our crops fast enough, we might just manage to stay ahead of the locusts.

The divine longing for trust can be satisfied only by practicing the heavenly virtue of *generosity*. Generosity (aka *charity*) is the ability to share what we have, both as an act of faith and as a sign of our hope in God's Providence. When we practice generosity, we trust that God will supply all that we need and that there is nothing to fear.

Gluttony

Gluttony is a distortion of the divine longing for *well-being*, that is, the desire for mental, physical, and spiritual integration. Jesus bore witness to this divine longing for well-being through his extensive ministry of healing both body and soul. In this life, the divine longing for well-being empowers us to live a healthy and whole life in balance. It facilitates our divinization by seeing to the development and ultimate perfection of every part of ourselves—body, mind, and spirit. Gluttony distorts the divine desire for wholeness in two ways.

First, gluttony tells us that feeling full of food and/or drink is an adequate substitute for living a healthy, balanced life. Stress-eating, overindulging with drink or drugs, or using other things to fill up our senses—all of this is an attempt to anesthetize ourselves against disorder and chaos in other parts of our lives. It convinces us that "treating" ourselves or indulging ourselves is the same thing as caring for our lives and ourselves.

The second way that gluttony can distort our divine longing for well-being is by leading us to seek to achieve wholeness by obsessing over the kinds of foods we eat or being overly particular about the way our food is prepared. St. Thomas Aquinas called this second type of gluttony *studiose,* the tendency to be overly fussy, particular, or precious about what we eat.

Good nutrition is important, but the belief that we can be saved by how, how much, and what we consume can become seriously problematic. The divine longing for well-being can be satisfied only by practicing the heavenly virtue of *temperance,* which is the ability to pursue and use all good things—not just food—in a healthy way that promotes the wholeness and balance for which we all ache.

Lust

Lust is a distortion of the divine longing for *communion,* the desire for intimate connection, to know and be known by another. God said, "It is not good that the man should be alone" (Gn 2:18). We were created for intimate communion, and we cannot be satisfied if we are cut off from the authentic love of both God and others. In this life, the divine longing for communion helps us create deep, intimate, and rewarding relationships. It facilitates our divinization by making us long for ultimate communion with the God who made us and calls us to him. The spirit of lust lies to us, telling us that true communion is unnecessary; rather, lust whispers that it is enough to create a connection with another person that is often just skin-deep. Lust ignores the call to soulful intimacy we were created to enjoy. It causes us to settle for the illusion of connection.

Our divine longing for communion can be satisfied only by practicing the heavenly virtue of *chastity*. Most people think chastity is limited to what some parents tell their children: "Don't have sex until you're married, or else!" But that's not true. Practicing chastity in the larger sense is trying to love every person in your life rightly. Chastity enables us to be as fully loving as might be appropriate with everyone with whom we have a relationship—not just our romantic partner. In general, chastity is the virtue that stops us from seeing people as a means to an end instead of as persons who have a right to be treated with love and dignity.

The following table presents an at-a-glance overview of how the seven deadly sins, the seven divine longings, and the seven heavenly virtues go together.

THIS DEADLY SIN . . .	DISTORTS THE DIVINE LONGING FOR . . .	WHICH CAN BE FULFILLED ONLY BY THIS HEAVENLY VIRTUE
Pride	Abundance	Humility
Envy	Dignity	Kindness
Wrath	Justice	Patience
Sloth	Peace	Diligence/Fortitude
Greed	Trust	Generosity/Charity
Gluttony	Well-being	Temperance
Lust	Communion	Chastity

The Divine Longings: A Shift in Focus

Viewing our desires as expressions of the seven divine longings enables us to see that giving in to sin is really not glamorous or fulfilling. In fact, it is a distraction from the authentic fulfillment of our deepest desires—desires that point to eternal realities. Likewise, understanding the seven divine longings invigorates our understanding of goodness. We don't practice the seven heavenly virtues just so we might avoid some existential spanking from our transcendent parent figure. We practice them so that we might finally, after all our seeking, find true satisfaction of the seven divine longings in a manner that enables us to fulfill our destiny to become gods through God's grace. Any goodness that results is the fruit, not the object, of this effort and better reflects the working of God's grace in us than it does a badge of honor that we pin on ourselves as a sign of our personal quest for spiritual superiority.

I Do Not Condemn You

When Jesus said to the adulterous woman, "Neither do I condemn you" (Jn 8:11), he was speaking to each of us. Too many people see the Christian walk as a lifelong attempt to avoid God's big, wagging, heavenly finger—as a series of "thou shalt not's" that must be scrupulously avoided if we are ever even to hope to pass muster. The Christian walk is none of these things. As Pope Benedict XVI observed, Christianity in general and Catholicism in particular has to be more than "a collection of prohibitions" (Spiegel Online International, 2006). The Christian walk is a call to fulfillment. It is a path to discovering that God is speaking to us through our desires, and that those same longings that have so often led us down false paths can, with the help of God's grace, be engines that drive our deification. In the words of Pope Benedict XVI,

> We must not forget that the dynamism of desire is always open to redemption. . . . We all, moreover, need to set out on the path of purification and healing of desire. We are pilgrims, heading for the heavenly homeland. . . . [The pilgrimage of desire] is not, then, about suffocating the longing that dwells in the heart of man, but about freeing it, so that it can reach its true height (2012).

It is my hope that, by discovering the seven divine longings of your heart, you will be set free to confront your brokenness in a new light. I hope that you can begin to leave behind the condemnation and suffocation of your past spiritual efforts and take up a new and easier yoke by which you learn to befriend your desires. The path God has set before you, even though it has its challenges, is not meant to be a path of punishment, rejection, failure, and scolding, but rather a path of fulfillment, acceptance, victory, and encouragement toward your heavenly destiny in Christ.

Chapter Three

Set Free from Struggle:
The Secret of the Imperfect Mystic

Let souls who are striving for perfection . . .
distinguish themselves by boundless trust in My
mercy. I myself will attend to the sanctification
of such souls. I will provide them with
everything they will need to attain sanctity.
—*St. Faustina,* Diary of Saint Maria Faustina
Kowalska: Divine Mercy in My Soul

In the last chapter you discovered how seeking to fulfill the seven divine longings of your heart can enable you to stop running from sin and instead begin running toward abundance and deification.

Even though this renewed focus can make our spiritual walk infinitely less burdensome, we will still struggle. Sometimes we will even stumble and fall. Most people respond poorly to failure, especially when we fail in our spiritual walk. We become consumed with neurotic guilt and self-hatred. We feel that the harder we are on ourselves, the more seriously we are taking our personal growth.

Know this: When we fail, as we inevitably will, God does not desire our guilt. In such times, his only wish is that we lay aside our fruitless striving and place ourselves in the loving care of the Divine Physician so that he may complete in us what we find ourselves incapable of healing on our own. To do this, to set ourselves free from our self-hatred and criticism, we must embrace the mystic's approach to imperfection.

Struggle and the Mystic

Recall that every Christian is called to be a mystic, that is, a person who is capable of seeing God moving behind the mundane and even profane events of our everyday lives. Previously, we focused on the unique relationship the mystic has with desire and how all of our desires—including our darkest longings—reveal something about God's infinite love for us and his incredible plans for us.

When confronted by spiritual struggles, mystics are able to resist the temptation to surrender to neurotic guilt and, instead, rejoice in the abundant mercy of God *especially* when they have made a terrific hash of things.

I've Fallen and I Can't Get Up!

Satan does not want us to become the gods that God intends us to be. So, as we discovered in the last chapter, his first tactic is to completely obscure the path of deification revealed through the seven divine longings. But a second way he plots against our success is by causing us to lose sight of God's grace when we fall. He hopes that he can persuade us to keep lying in the mud of our own pathetic brokenness, and that he can prevent us from getting back up again. But God will raise you up if you let him!

Peter could walk on the water as long as he kept his eyes

on Christ, but as soon as he looked at the wind and waves instead, he began to drown (Mt 14:28-31). The same is true for us. When we fail, as we inevitably will, we have a choice to make: Will we focus in disgust on our failings and brokenness? Or will we turn our eyes to the merciful face of God and find the strength to laugh good-naturedly at our feebleness while rejoicing in the abundant, loving mercy of God, who has at his disposal the power of the universe to raise us out of the ditch we've dug for ourselves?

I Will Boast of My Weakness!

> How happy I am to see myself imperfect and be in need of God's mercy.
>
> *—St. Thérèse of the Child Jesus*

Recognizing that it is the depth of our relationship with God, not our goodness, that propels us down the path of deification, the mystic realizes that failure is an opportunity to encounter grace. St. Paul speaks of this in the Second Letter to the Corinthians:

> Therefore, that I might not become too elated, a thorn in the flesh was given to me, an angel of Satan, to beat me, to keep me from being too elated. Three times I begged the Lord about this, that it might leave me, but he said to me, "My grace is sufficient for you, for power is made perfect in weakness." I will rather boast most gladly of my weaknesses, in order that the power of Christ may dwell with

me. Therefore, I am content with weaknesses, insults, hardships, persecutions, and constraints, for the sake of Christ; for when I am weak, then I am strong (12:7-10).

How many of us can relate to Paul's frustration? He begs God to take away this struggle, this . . . *thing* that he finds frustrating about himself, *and still it remains.* So what does God tell him to do? To beat himself up? To despair that he will never be good enough? God challenges Paul to abandon his desire to prove himself worthy through his pathetic efforts and asks him instead to surrender into a deeper relationship with God and a more intense encounter with God's transforming love.

Earlier, in his first letter to the church in Corinth, St. Paul points directly at what I am calling the divine longings of the human heart when he says,

Therefore, do not make any judgment before the appointed time, until the Lord comes, *for he will bring to light what is hidden in darkness and will manifest the motives of our hearts, and then everyone will receive praise from God* (1 Cor 4:5 emphasis mine).

Most people read this passage and think that St. Paul is referring to God exposing the darkness of our hearts, that he is talking about our sin. But why, having exposed our deepest sins, would God praise us?

He praises us not because he reveals our sins—those are obvious—but because he reveals the divine longings behind those sins, which are praiseworthy! Paul reminds us, after all, to rejoice in God's power to reclaim the godly treasure buried under our brokenness and to help us find fulfillment and divinization despite ourselves.

This is how the mystic faces his failures. Not with shame. Not with condemnation. Not with self-hatred or crippling guilt, but with the knowledge that he is being invited to draw closer to God so that God may instruct his heart in love and transform him from the inside out. When we surrender our pathetic efforts to transform ourselves, we discover God's power to transform us.

So why is it so difficult to overcome our struggles by our own effort? And how can we get to the place where we are no longer tormented by our struggles and are instead able to surrender ourselves to the transforming power of God's love? The practical answer to both questions may come to us from a surprising source—neuroscience.

Grace on the Brain

Neuroscience teaches us that the brain locks down when it experiences even short-term stress (Baram, 2008). Stress triggers both chemical and neurological changes that make it difficult for nerve cells to grow and new connections to be formed in the brain. These connections are an essential part of hardwiring—so to speak—the experiences we've had so that we can learn from those experiences, retain those lessons, and benefit from them in the future. This tendency for the brain to lock down during stress protects us from being traumatized from bad experiences in the short term, but it also accounts for our tendency to make the same foolish mistakes over and over again. Neurotic guilt, judgmentalism, anger, blame, and shame all impair our ability to process new experiences, integrate new information, and create change. When we feel attacked, even by ourselves, the brain clamps down as a way of freezing out the threat and preventing us from being negatively impacted by an experience deemed to be contrary to our best interest. When this happens, we get tunnel vision and we shut out everything that doesn't relate to seeking immediate relief from our pain. We focus on "getting through" the experience, not learning from it. We're reactive rather than responsive. Rather than feeling effective, connected to others, and able to grow and adapt, we feel powerless, isolated, self-pitying, and prone to self-indulgence as a way of anesthetizing ourselves from the pain of the moment.

By contrast, the brain is most open to change when we are experiencing the state of mind produced when four qualities—represented by the acronym COAL—are present: *curiosity, openness, acceptance,* and *love* (Siegel 2007; 2012).

I want to explain what it means to approach oneself and one's failings with the mind-set that enables us to see God moving behind even our failings, but first I want to address two objections that I imagine some people might have to COAL. First, *shouldn't* we feel guilty when we do something wrong? And, second, why should anyone interested in spiritual growth care one whit about the brain?

Is There No Place for Guilt?

Of course we should feel guilty when we do something wrong. But there are two kinds of guilt. The first is a loving correction from the Holy Spirit. When we experience godly guilt, we recognize that we have committed some offense, but the Holy Spirit simultaneously points us toward what we can do to try to resolve the problem. With godly guilt, the awareness of our wrongdoing is followed immediately by the *peace of knowing that God will help us make things right.* The person experiencing this type of guilt actually experiences a sense of consolation rather than a sense of condemnation. *"I do not condemn you"* (Jn 8:11).

By contrast, neurotic guilt causes us to wallow in our wrongdoing without any plan or hope of making things better. St. Ignatius of Loyola considers this type of neurotic guilt a "desolation," or a temptation from an evil spirit that makes it more difficult for us to draw close to God or become the people we were created to be.

Unfortunately, after rejecting this experience of guilt as unhealthy, a lot of people engage in an equally foolish acceptance of all their imperfections. They think, "Well, making myself miserable about all my failings didn't work, so now I'll just tell myself how awesome I am in spite of all my failings!" This is what many people imagine when I talk about adopting an attitude of curiosity, openness, acceptance, and love toward oneself. They initially think I am telling them to embrace the behavior of the addict who never met an impulse he didn't like. Of course, this is not what I am advocating at all. But more on that in a minute.

Guilt and the Mystical Brain

The second objection many people raise to the concept of COAL is, "Why should we care about the brain?" After all, this is a book on spirituality. The answer is simple. In his theology of the body, St. John Paul the Great tells us that by prayerfully contemplating the design of the body, we can learn a great deal about God's plan for our life and relationships: "*The fact that theology also includes the body should not astonish or surprise anyone who is conscious of the mystery and reality of the Incarnation*" (Pope John Paul II, 2006).

Remember, the mystic sees God at work behind all the mundane and even the profane aspects of everyday life. From this mystical perspective we see that biology itself is a theology. We are made in God's image and likeness, and his fingerprints are all over our design. The more we understand how God has made us, the more easily we can develop holistic approaches to cooperating with his grace so that we can train our biological impulses, drives, and desires instead of warring against them. Had St. Francis of Assisi had the information you will discover over the next few pages, perhaps he would have had no need to repent at the end of his life for referring to his body as "Brother Ass." Too late he proclaimed on his deathbed, "*Rejoice, brother body, and forgive me, for behold, now I gladly fulfill your desires, and gladly hasten to attend to thy complaints*" (Wiseman, 2001).

COAL: The Fuel for Change

As I mentioned above, neuroscience suggests that our brains become more receptive to changing when we adopt an attitude of *curiosity, openness, acceptance,* and *love* toward life in general, but especially toward our failings (Siegel, 2007; 2012). Let's briefly consider how fostering each of these qualities can help us cooperate more effectively with God's transformative grace.

Curiosity

Curiosity refers to a genuine desire to understand. The opposite of curiosity is judgmentalism. When most of us fail, we criticize and shame ourselves. This is Satan's way of preventing us from asking the deeper questions our failings invite us to consider, namely, "What hurt am I trying to address with this behavior?" "What divine longing is God trying to fulfill?" "What is the godly motivation behind my fallen choices?" Satan does not want us to ask these questions. He would prefer that we remain ignorant because the answers to these questions point to the seven divine longings, whose true fulfillment propels us toward deification. When we respond to life with curiosity, we take a gentle, questioning posture toward ourselves. When we can approach our brokenness with curiosity, we are open to learning something, and God will teach us. By contrast, judgmentalism slams the door in both God's and our own faces. We have nothing to learn. We already have everything figured out—and everything is bad.

Jimmy has always struggled with procrastination—a form of sloth. "I used to beat up on myself about it. When I was a kid, my parents used to get on me about not living up to their expectations and cutting corners. As an adult, I would often end up showing up late for things, or getting things done at the last minute, or not getting them done at all. I even lost jobs over it. Some people said I must have adult ADHD, and I started taking medication for it, but I always felt like there was something more to it. It wasn't just that I couldn't focus. I actually felt myself fighting against getting better. I resisted being pinned down to commitments. I refused to even try to keep a schedule. I wouldn't write things down even if my life depended on it. It was weird.

"I used to beat up on myself and say I was just lazy, that people couldn't count on me. I was talking about it in confession once, though, and the priest asked me a weird question. He said, 'Have you ever asked what God is trying to teach you through your tendency to avoid responsibility?' I thought he was crazy at the time. I told him that I had no idea. He let it go and gave me absolution.

"But afterward his question kept nagging at me. Eventually I took it to prayer. I went before the Blessed Sacrament and I asked God to help me see what this whole thing was about. After a few minutes, it all kind of just clicked in my head. When I was a kid, my brother was sick all the time. He had a genetic disorder that landed him in the hospital periodically. He died when he was seven and I was ten. I just remembered how, when he would get sick, I used to try so hard to take care of my parents and stuff. They would be so worried about him. I'd do the dishes and dust and clean up and all that. My parents would barely notice, but I didn't care. I just wanted them to not worry. Then, after he died, I just stopped doing anything. I never thought of it before, but it occurred to me that, for me, committing to things, 'being responsible,' brought back all that worry and grief about my brother. At first I thought I was being stupid, that I was making excuses, but then I thought, 'What if there's something to this?' It's not an excuse. I still needed to change, but it was a step forward for me to realize that my laziness was really an attempt to avoid dragging up a lot of bad stuff.

"After that time in adoration, I watched when those feelings came over me the strongest. It usually seemed that I got the laziest when I was stressed or worried about something. I would just shut down. I started paying closer attention, and when I felt the shutdown feelings coming, I would pray and ask God for the grace to remember that I didn't need to run away from stress anymore, that I wasn't a kid and my world wasn't going to come crashing down on me at any minute just because I was feeling overwhelmed. Things didn't change overnight, but with time I really saw God delivering me from my fear of responsibility and commitment. It's ironic, but only when I stopped trying so hard was I able to get over this. God didn't want me to fix myself. He wanted me to trust in his love and mercy and let my struggles draw me closer to him so I could be healed by his love."

By rejecting judgmentalism in favor of a spirit of curiosity, Jimmy was able to see God moving behind his brokenness and to receive the key to his transformation. While he still found that he a lot of work to do, he felt a sense of hope that hadn't seemed possible before. Instead of guilt and self-recrimination, he experienced love, mercy, and deeper union with God. In sum, when we engage our *curiosity,* we are able to ask God the questions that need to be asked, and to find the answers God is trying to communicate to us. Curiosity makes us receptive to what God is attempting to do in us.

Openness

Openness is the second quality that makes transformation possible. It is the opposite of close-mindedness. While engaging our curiosity enables us to ask questions about our motivations, being open helps us to receive, with an open heart, the answers that come to us. In the preceding case study, Jimmy struggled with openness. When the memories of his behavior during the time of his brother's illness emerged, he told himself that he was just being stupid and making excuses. God had to nudge Jimmy through that initial close-mindedness so that Jimmy would be willing to meditate on what God was trying to reveal to him.

I often encounter this close-mindedness in my clients. Memories or insights come forward and they bat them out of the way. "That's ridiculous!" they'll say. Or "That couldn't have anything to do with this!" They may even be right. But being unwilling to consider the possibility that God is revealing something to us is simply foolish. Before we reject a memory or insight, we should at least take it to prayer. Our minds are not random. They are orderly. They recall things for a reason. If I am prompted to recall a thought, insight, or memory while I am prayerfully reflecting on some struggle in my life, then it is worth meditating on whether there is at least a tenuous connection. It can be helpful to pray further about those connections even if we ultimately reject them as irrelevant. Being open does not require us to accept, as gospel, every silly thought that pops into our heads, but it does require us to admit that there might be more to our initial thoughts than meets the eye. Our prayerful openness gives God the chance to develop the pictures that begin to emerge under the light of his grace.

Acceptance

Acceptance is the third quality that facilitates spiritual transformation. Although acceptance is the opposite of self-criticism, it is not the same thing as approval. Imagine that you are a service technician called to repair a broken piece of complicated machinery. You arrive at the job site and take it all in. When you see what is wrong, how do you react? Do you take it personally? Of course not. Instead, you accept things for what they are and patiently set about addressing the problem. You know the more impatient you are, the more likely it is you'll just end up breaking something else and making the job harder.

When we are refocusing on the process of repairing ourselves, acceptance is the quality by which we trust that "God's grace is sufficient" and rest in him when we find our efforts are not up to the task at hand. Yes, of course we have to make what changes we can in our life, but, like the service technician, we must realize that the job takes what it takes. Any attempt to rush things just mucks up the process.

Acceptance does not mean that we rejoice in our brokenness as the addict does. It simply means that we are willing to take, at face value, what appears to be wrong and what needs to be done to address it. We address what we can, *and we rejoice in what we find ourselves unable to do,* knowing that God's infinite mercy will make up the difference.

Love

Finally, we come to the last virtue in our acronym COAL, *love.* To love someone means that we are committed to working for their good. Loving ourselves means being similarly committed to working for our own good. St. John Paul the Great's theology of the body teaches that authentic love must be free, total, faithful, and fruitful (2006). The pope is speaking in the context of the love between man and woman, but I think these terms can be applied to a healthy love of self as well. What would it look like for us to have a free, total, faithful, and fruitful love of self? Consider the following.

I will love myself freely. I commit to working for my good without reservation, without grumbling. I will not hold back in my efforts to challenge myself to open my heart wide to receive the transformation God wishes to give me and to cooperate to the best of my ability with his grace at all times.

I will love myself totally. While there are parts of myself that are hard to like, I will not turn away from them. I will celebrate the fact that I am fearfully and wonderfully made (Ps 139:14), that I am good (Gn 1:31), and that God has great things in store for me (1 Cor 2:9). I will fearlessly cooperate with God's grace and strive for greatness so that every part of me, especially the parts of me I like the least, may be transformed and bear witness to the wonders God can do.

I will love myself faithfully. Even on the days when I want to give up on myself, I will continue to fight the good fight (2 Tim 4:7). I will reject self-criticism and false guilt and any movement of the spirit that tries to separate me from either the love of God or his ability to fulfill the incredible plans he has for my life (2 Cor 10:5). On the days when I can no longer believe in myself, I will cling to the knowledge that God believes in me. On the days when I cannot count on my own strength, I will rely on his. I will not beat myself up for my weakness. Rather, I will boast in the power of God (1 Cor 1:31) to raise me up from weakness to glory.

I will love myself fruitfully. I will rejoice in the good things

God does in and through me. I will look for ways to be a blessing to others. I will share the blessings God has given me, and I will proclaim the good he has done for me (Ps 116:12) that others might be inspired by the wonders God is working in me.

Be Not Afraid!

This is the attitude we aspiring mystics must adopt as we face the darkest parts of ourselves and our frustrated efforts to heal. We will not give in to fear, anger, or condemnation. Instead we will practice the *curiosity, openness, acceptance,* and free, total, faithful, and fruitful *love* that will enable us to rejoice in our failings because of God's immeasurable mercy and love, and, in turn, we will be transformed by the power of his infinite grace.

Become What You Are!

St. John Paul the Great was fond of telling the people in his audiences, "Become what you are!" What did he mean? Only that we should spend our lives becoming the gods whom God sees when he looks at us, the gods we are meant to be through God's grace.

Having laid out a system that allows us to put in proper context our desires and our attempts to fulfill them, we are ready to begin—or more likely continue—the work of becoming the divinized person God is telling us that we can become if only we will trust him and let him show us the way. The remainder of this book will look more specifically at ways that you can fulfill each of the divine longings, namely,

> the divine longing for abundance
> the divine longing for dignity
> the divine longing for justice
> the divine longing for peace
> the divine longing for trust
> the divine longing for well-being
> the divine longing for communion

As we look at each of these hidden, sacred longings, it is my hope that you will discover how your desires can empower you to cooperate with God's plan to transform you, through his grace, into everything you are destined to be. May God bless and sustain you on this journey through grace.

Chapter Four

Satisfying the Divine Longing for Abundance

I came that they might have life and
have it more abundantly!
—*John 10:10*

When I ask my clients what they hope to get out of counseling, the number one answer is "I just want to be happy."

In our quest to be happy, we all tend to stumble around in the dark chasing after so many things, few of which give us real joy. But there is good news. As much as you desire happiness, God longs even more to fill your heart with a soul-satisfying joy designed to exceed your greatest expectations.

In this chapter, you will discover the source of authentic happiness, how happiness relates to the divine longing for abundance, and how to avoid the most common errors people make as they strive to fulfill this longing. Finally, I will lead you through an exercise that will help you overcome the obstacles standing between you and the joy you seek.

God Cares About Your Happiness

At the heart of the many promises God makes to humankind is the fact that God cares deeply about your happiness. St. John Paul the Great proclaimed, *"People are made for happiness.*

Rightly, then, you thirst for happiness. Christ has the answer to this desire of yours. But he asks you to trust him" (2002).

Pope Benedict XVI agreed with his predecessor, asserting, *"God wants us to be happy always. He knows us and he loves us. If we allow the love of Christ to change our heart, then we can change the world. This is the secret of authentic happiness"* (Zenit, 2012).

Likewise, in 2014 Pope Francis gave an interview in which he outlined a ten-point plan for building happiness involving, among other items, recommendations such as acceptance (defined largely as we discussed earlier with COAL), sharing oneself with others, and making time for both family and quiet reflection (Pentin, 2014). Of course, most important of all, Jesus proclaimed his desire to teach us the path to abundance in the Scripture passage that begins this chapter.

The truth is, God has an incredible plan in store for your happiness in this life and the next. You cannot begin to imagine the joy God desires for you. As St. Paul writes, "Eye has not seen, and ear has not heard . . . what God has prepared for those who love him" (1 Cor 2:9).

The Divine Longing for Abundance

If God desires our happiness so much, why is it so difficult for us to achieve satisfaction? Perhaps it is because we are aiming at the wrong target.

Psychology reveals that there are two kinds of happiness: hedonic (pleasure-driven) happiness, and abundance (meaning-driven) happiness (Ryan and Deci, 2001). *Pleasure-driven happiness* comes from seeking enjoyment and avoiding stressful situations. *Abundance happiness* (also referred to as "authentic happiness") is the soul-satisfying joy that one experiences from living a good life (Seligman, 2002). Research shows that while both types of happiness can feel pleasant, pleasure-seeking happiness tends to be very fleeting, transient, and unstable while abundance happiness is constant, consistent, and can bring deep inner joy even through the ups and downs of life (Seligman, 2002). Surprisingly, the difference between these two types of happiness is bone-deep.

One fascinating study examined how these two types of happiness affect the way genes are expressed (i.e., turn on or off based on environmental cues). It found that people who are oriented toward a more pleasure-based pursuit of happiness exhibited gene expression that was consistent with a high inflammatory response in the body (think joint swelling and other pain) as well as suppressed antibody and antiviral responses in the body (leaving them more susceptible to disease and infection). By contrast, the people who pursued happiness by living a good life exhibited gene expression consistent with a low inflammatory response and high antibody and antiviral production (Wheeler, 2013). The researchers point out that it was not the genes that influenced the type of happiness the participants chased after. Rather, it was the type of happiness the participants pursued that caused the particular genetic response.

In his theology of the body, St. John Paul the Great teaches that by prayerful contemplation of the way our bodies are designed, we can discover important things about God's plan for a fulfilling life and relationships. God has hardwired our bodies to crave abundance so that we might ultimately find the path to fulfillment and divinization through his love. It is this hardwired, bone-deep, universally human ache for fulfillment that I call the divine longing for abundance, which is the first and most important of the seven longings of the human heart.

Defining "the Good Life"

What does satisfying the divine longing for abundance actually require of us? Research reveals that abundance can be defined by the pursuit of three qualities: *meaningfulness, intimacy*, and *virtue*.

When we try to bring *meaningfulness* into our lives, we use our gifts, talents, and abilities in a manner that is both enriching to us and a blessing to others. We can pursue meaningfulness in bigger ways, for instance, by choosing a career or volunteer work in which we help make the world a better place. We can also pursue meaningfulness in smaller ways, for instance, by doing our best to apply ourselves fully and creatively to whatever mundane tasks fill our day instead of just cutting corners to get the job done.

Living with meaningfulness is akin to what St. John Paul the Great refers to as "self-donation," a kind of heroic generosity that asks how I might use whatever God has given me—not just my talents, gifts, and abilities, but my body as well—to make others' lives better or more joyful. Living a meaningful life contributes to our sense of abundance by helping us feel that we matter, that we have what it takes to make a difference in the lives of others, that our very presence can be a gift.

Intimacy refers to our ability to work for deep, close, healthy, and supportive relationships. Think of intimacy as a unit of measure for love, like gallons for liquid or inches for length. If love is a body of water, intimacy tells us whether that body of water is a puddle or an ocean. People who pursue intimacy work hard to draw closer to others in healthy ways that allow them to experience their relationships as a gift. In his theology of the body, St. John Paul the Great reminds us that we are called to create "communities of love" where we and the people in our lives are mutually committed to working for one another's good. People who pursue intimacy make a priority of both seeking deeper communion with the healthy people in their lives and setting boundaries that might help more difficult relationships to become healthier in time. Intimacy contributes to our sense of abundance by making us part of a community where we are loved, cherished, and valued as persons. The human person is relational by nature. The pursuit of intimacy helps us make certain that our relational selves are as healthy as they can be.

Finally, *virtue* refers to our ability to take whatever life throws at us and use it to become better, stronger, healthier people—more integrated examples of all the things we claim to stand for or believe in. The word "virtue" comes from the Latin words for "strength" and "manliness." Virtue is the quality that allows us to take everything life gives to us, even the challenges, and ask, "How can I respond to this in such a way that growth and good may come of it?" Virtue contributes to our sense of abundance by empowering us to see that there is no such thing as failure or hardship. Rather, every experience I have is another opportunity to discover how I might live a full, rich, life rooted in wisdom and strength.

Abundance Through Community

Perhaps most important, the pursuit of *meaningfulness, intimacy,* and *virtue* helps us to achieve abundance by enabling us to rediscover our essential human need for connection with others. Remember that in Genesis God says that it is not good for us to be alone (see Gn 2:18). It is *our ability to connect with others that enables us to be fully human.* Fostering meaning-fulness in our lives facilitates this connection by motivating us to use our gifts for the good of others. The quality of inti-macy emphasizes the importance of building a healthy com-munity of support so that we can become everything we were created to be and help others do the same. Even virtue orients us toward others, by both helping us be more open to what we can learn from them and having our experiences serve as an inspiration to them.

Both Christian tradition and psychological research show us that the keys to experiencing abundance on every level of our personhood—emotionally, spiritually, and even physically—are found in choosing to pursue *meaningfulness, intimacy,* and *virtue* in everything we do. This is the happi-ness that God wants to give you, the happiness you long for in your bones. The authentic, bone-deep joy that comes from living life more abundantly (Jn 10:10).

Do By Self!

But even when we realize that the happiness our hearts long for is best achieved by pursuing abundance, it can still be chal-lenging to discover and remain on the pathways that lead to it. What is the secret? St. John Paul the Great pointed to the answer in the second part of his quote on happiness, which I referenced earlier in this chapter: *"Christ has the answer to this desire of yours. But he asks you to trust him"* (2002).

Although Jesus Christ certainly deserves our trust, most of us do not have an easy time trusting him. We have a hard enough time trusting the friends we can see, much less the God we can't see. We insist that we, and we alone, have the right to determine what will make us happy. Like the tod-dler who, in his mind, is much more competent than reality would suggest, we all want to "do by self!" We fear that if we trust anyone, most of all God, we will be condemned to a life of lonely, miserable servitude. Oh, sure, if we listen to others we may become good. If we listen to God we might become holy. But we strongly doubt that we will be fulfilled and happy.

As you discovered in chapter 2, the assertion that we alone can find our way to happiness is at the very heart of the sin of pride. Christianity considers pride to be the deadliest of deadly sins because it thwarts the very deepest of all the long-ings of the human heart—our divine longing for abundance. Pride compels us to hoard our gifts and attempt to find our own paths to abundance, but abundance can be achieved only by being humble enough to realize that I do not have all the answers and my gifts are not sufficient on their own. Achiev-ing abundance requires participating in community, sharing my gifts with others and benefiting from the gifts of others, as well as recognizing that I have a lot to learn about life and what living life to the full requires. God wants us to be happy, and he offers a vision of happiness that will truly satisfy us in both this life and the next, but because we are afraid to "trust Christ," we end up running around chasing after lesser joys that can never satisfy us. Not really.

Pride: Settling for Less

When we give in to pride, we adopt the attitude that "if we want to be happy, we have to take care of ourselves." Because pride compels us to rely on our own limited power, we often feel that our lives lack the *meaning* they should have. Because pride tells us we don't need God or others, *intimacy* escapes us and we feel isolated. Because pride tells us that we have nothing to learn from life, we fail to develop the *virtues* that help us experience both the ups and downs of life as the gifts they truly are. As a result, rather than experiencing the abundance God wants to teach us to experience, we are forced to settle for less. When we live without *meaningfulness, intimacy,* and *virtue,* our lives become smaller and smaller as our choices close in on us, we push people away, and our attempts at self-comforting fail us.

The conscious and intentional pursuit of *meaningfulness, intimacy* and *virtue* enables us to get the most out of every moment and come to value both ourselves and our life as they divine gifts they are meant to be.

Pride: I Will Not Serve!

Pride further corrupts our ability to pursue abundance by denying our radically communal nature. Pride says, "I will live my life for myself!" It echoes Satan's very own words at the dawn of time, *"Non serviam!" I will NOT serve!* Rather than inspiring us to use what we have to be a blessing to others, pride says that we should be the sole benefactors of any advantages we have been given. Instead of challenging us to see others as persons who have a right to be loved and from whom we may learn much, pride orients us to seeing others as inferior objects that have value only to the degree that they can serve us or fulfill our pleasure. Instead of leading us toward learning and using the lessons life can teach us, pride tells us that life has nothing to teach us, that we are perfectly perfect just the way we are, and that we have nothing to do in response to life but be whomever we care to be. But as the study we discussed earlier shows, the hedonistic pursuits pride inspires undermine the emotional, psychological, and even physical abundance we seek.

Humility: The Source of Abundance

> The most powerful weapon to conquer the devil is humility. For, as he does not know at all how to employ it, neither does he know how to defend himself from it.
>
> —*St. Vincent de Paul*

> Humility is not thinking less of ourselves; it is thinking of ourselves less.
>
> —*C. S. Lewis*

Humility is the heavenly virtue that is classically seen as an antidote to pride. Unfortunately, humility is often equated with tearing oneself down, with diminishing oneself. We think of being humble as the opposite of being proud of ourselves and taking joy in our accomplishments or our other gifts.

As I have noted previously, pride is not the "sin" of being pleased with yourself or your gifts, nor is it the putative "virtue" of failing to rejoice in those gifts. If you give your child a gift, you expect your child to be excited about it, don't you? How disappointed would you be if your child received your gift with little more than a grim nod out of fear of seeming too happy? Jesus tells us that if we who are imperfect can give our children good things, how much more can our Father in heaven do so for his children (Mt 7:11)? If that's true, how much more do you think God wants his children to be excited about and rejoice in the gifts, talents, treasures, and beauty that he has given them? When the psalmist contemplates the wonders of his body, he does not say, "Um, thanks, God. I guess it's okay." No! He proclaims, "I praise you, Lord, for I am fearfully and wonderfully made!" (Ps 139:14). When was the last time you looked in the mirror and said something like that about what you saw? Was King David being prideful when he sang this incredible song? Of course not.

"Humility" shares the same Latin root as the word "humus," or soil. Which is not to say that humility is the same thing as mere dirt. As any gardener knows, humus is rich, fertile soil. It produces much fruit and many flowers. Humus is the good patch of earth one can rejoice in!

So if living with humility does not mean beating up on oneself for allegedly spiritual purposes, what is humility really, and how does it both counteract pride and help us achieve abundance? Recall that pride denies our radical communal nature. It claims that I have no obligation to share my gifts with others, nothing to learn from others, and no need for my life to be complicated by intimate relationships with others. By contrast, humility is the virtue that makes me radically receptive to being with, learning from, and sharing myself and my gifts with others. This is true even of the qualities such as beauty, achievement, or status that are associated with the type of pride known as vanity or vainglory. The sin of vanity or vainglory isn't the sin of dressing well or rejoicing over one's achievements. It is the sin of *lording* one's appearance or accomplishments *over others* instead of using one's appearance to facilitate healthy social interaction or one's accomplishments to be a blessing. Even in these instances, pride is the sin of saying "I will not serve."

As I shared earlier, abundance can be satisfied only by the active pursuit of *meaningfulness, intimacy,* and *virtue*. Humility facilitates *meaningfulness* by making me *want* to give my gifts and talents to others. Humility says, "If what I have can be a help to you, please let me share it with you."

Humility facilitates *intimacy* by inspiring us to say, "You are important to me. I want to see the truth, goodness, and beauty in everything you find true, good, and beautiful. Teach me to see the world as you do!"

Humility facilitates *virtue* by inviting us to ask ourselves, "What can life teach me today?" Humility is the virtue that makes us useful to God and enables us to be a profound blessing to others. It is such a powerful virtue that, in the words of St. Teresa of Avila, "There is more value in a little study of humility and in a single act of it than in all the knowledge in the world" (Clores, 2002).

Scripture reminds us that we can never seem to find the right time to act, the right path to take, the right things to do that will make us happy (Eccl 3). There comes a point when all the things pride tells us to chase leave us cold. Humility facilitates abundance by placing our hearts in a receptive mode. *We* cannot find the right time to act, but God can. If we are willing to learn, God will show us how to walk the paths of both *authentic,* bone-deep happiness and divinization at the same time. Humility leads us to the surprising discovery that it is possible to be both authentically happy *and* holy!

Humility and Abundance in Action

It's one thing to talk about how humility can facilitate abundance, but what does it look like in real life? Let's examine two examples:

"I'd like to understand my wife better," Jonathan said. "Marianne and I have been having a hard time of it the last couple of years. I haven't always been the best listener, but I think I'm finally in a place where I can hear the things she needs to tell me."

At first, Jonathan came to counseling because his wife threatened to leave him if he didn't, but he's been an active participant since day one. "I convinced myself that everything I was doing I was doing for them—the work, the long hours, the late nights. Even the time I spent on my hobbies I told myself was so that I could be more present to them, but counseling has been a real eye-opening experience for me. I used to just write Marianne off as a nag, but since we've been in counseling, I really see that her asking me to change how I spend my time isn't about her saying I'm screwing up or not good enough, but that it's really about her saying she loves me, misses me, and wants to spend time with me. I never really thought of it that way.

"She has said a lot of things that were hard to hear, but I'm glad I've been listening better these last couple of weeks. I can tell Marianne feels more like I care, like I've really heard her. I think if we can just keep up being humble enough to learn from each other, we'll be okay."

Paige knows that she can't do everything by herself. She's a working mom who has limited time and energy. She knows a lot of other moms who feel very strongly that they have to prove that they can do it all. She used to be that way too, but she has learned that she can't do it all alone and that she shouldn't try. Her husband and her kids are there for her. She needed to learn to rely on them more.

At first it wasn't easy. Asking her husband, James, and her kids to help out more was a blow to her pride. And it was tough letting go of how things were done too. Paige can be a little particular at times. It's hard not to want things to be done "just so." But she realizes that her way isn't the only way, and as long as things get done, she is learning to be grateful for the support. She says, "It's been good to open up my heart and let other people help me. Sometimes my husband does things around the house differently than I do, but I've learned some good tips from him too. He wasn't really raised to help much around the house, so I kind of tended to discount his abilities before. I see now that he just needed me to let him know it was okay to help out. I guess we're learning from each other!"

Jonathan and Paige have both discovered small ways to practice humility. It hasn't been easy for either of them, and it has required them to grow in openness toward the people who share their lives. Nevertheless, as they have become more open, they have learned important things about themselves, about how to experience more intimacy and support from the people around them, and how to live more satisfying lives. Jonathan and Paige have both, in little ways, learned how to do what Christians call "dying to themselves." That is, they have discovered little ways to have the humility to accept that they need God and others to teach them how to live abundantly. Ironically, as terrifying as it sounds to die to oneself, Jonathan and Paige have found a more authentic, joyful, and *abundant* way of being by embracing humility and opening their hearts to others—even those with whom they don't see eye to eye.

Perhaps you have struggled with a tendency to close your ears and your heart to others. Perhaps you have tended to use your gifts to glorify yourself or unintentionally draw attention to your competence, skills, and gifts, as if you are better than those around you. Perhaps you have found it difficult to respond well to criticism, discuss mistakes, or listen to others' concerns without feeling like your own happiness is being threatened. If so, the following exercise can help you begin to free yourself from the bonds of pride and to embrace an authentic humility that helps you achieve abundance in this life and divinization in the next.

Satisfying the Divine Longing for Abundance: An Exercise

PRAY

Lord Jesus Christ,

I surrender my right to find my own way and I choose instead to follow your way. You have made me in your image and likeness. Father,

Son, and Holy Spirit, you defer to one another and reverence each other. Help me to follow your example in my life. Help me to remember that I can never understand myself or find true happiness if I keep myself apart from you or others. Help me to open my heart to the needs of others. Help me to be receptive to the concerns of others. Empower me to share my gifts with others. Give me your grace that I might embrace my need for you and for others in my life, and that by doing so I will be empowered to discover the path to abundance, perfection, and eternal life in you. Lead me and guide me. I am yours. Amen.

COAL: Fuel for Change

As you consider the ways you might be better able to satisfy the divine longing for abundance in your life, take a moment to consider how COAL can be the fuel for the changes you seek.

CURIOSITY AND OPENNESS

Ask yourself: Where did I learn that making myself open to serving and listening to the feelings and opinions of others was threatening?

> Who taught me this response?
>
> What situations impressed this lesson on me?
>
> Do I want to continue to allow these experiences to rule my life?

Do not judge or edit yourself. Receive your answers in a spirit of openness and grace.

ACCEPTANCE

Say, "These are the experiences that have shaped my struggle to satisfy my divine longing for abundance. I accept my past even as I accept God's call that I change and grow."

LOVE

Loving myself means working to become the person God wants me to be. I know that I can fulfill my deepest longing for abundance by responding with humility to the people and circumstances of my life.

> In those times when I feel self-protective or threatened, how could I respond in a manner that reflects the healthy humility described in this chapter?
>
> What obstacles would I have to overcome to achieve these goals?
>
> What help, resources, or support might I need to overcome these obstacles?
>
> Say, "I will love myself and accept God's love for me by choosing this path of humility over the temptation to pride."

Review these loving resolutions each morning. Imagine a time in the coming day when you might be tempted to pride. Imagine responding with humility instead. Ask for God's help to remember to respond with love in those times when your humility is tested.

Practicing Humility: Action Items

Living in humility promotes abundance by helping you cultivate meaningfulness, intimacy, and virtue. Reflect and respond to the following questions:

Meaningfulness results when we place our gifts at the service of others. What ways can you use your gifts to serve the people closest to you more effectively?

Intimacy results when we are willing to see the world through the eyes of others. In what situations will you strive to be more receptive to the experience/perspective of someone close to you?

Virtue results when we seek to learn what life is trying to teach us about ourselves through the challenges we face. What is life trying to teach you through the difficulties you are encountering in your present circumstances?

The Divine Longing for Abundance: A Promise

Throughout this chapter, we have examined the nature of the divine longing for abundance, the keys to achieving abundance, how pride distorts this longing, and, finally, how authentic humility enables us to open our hearts to learn the lessons God wants to teach us through both the experiences of our life and the lives of others.

As we conclude this chapter, I want to remind you once again how much God desires your wholeness and fulfillment by reminding you of the words of St. John Paul the Great:

"People are made for happiness. Rightly, then, you thirst for happiness. Christ has the answer to this desire of yours. But he asks you to trust him."

I pray that you will know the joy that comes from trusting Christ, the source of our abundance. For his greatest desire is to help you find fulfillment in this life in ways that will lead to your divinization in the next!

Chapter Five

Satisfying the Divine Longing for Dignity

Human personhood must be respected with a reverence
that is religious. When we deal with each other, we
should do so with the sense of awe that arises in the
presence of something holy and sacred. For that is what
human beings are: we are created in the image of God.

—*U.S. Conference of Catholic Bishops,*
Economic Justice for All

If you could only see how much you are worth in God's eyes!
Take a moment to imagine the person you love the most. Imagine all the reasons you love them, everything about them
that brings you joy. Do they really know how loved they are?
Wouldn't you give anything for them to know how precious,
how valuable, how important they are to you?

Jesus reminds us that everything we feel toward the ones
we love, everything that we desire to give to them, our heavenly Father desires for *us* a hundredfold (Mt 7:11). Each one of
us is of unfathomable worth and value in God's eyes. Our dignity is not rooted in what we do or accomplish or are capable
of. Our dignity is rooted in the fact that we are loved by God.

Let us explore the parable of the Pearl of Great Price (Mt
13:45-46) as a way of illustrating how God's plan to make us partakers in his divine nature is the most precious gift he can give
us. Specifically, I'd like to imagine us looking at this story from

God's point of view. In the story, a merchant finds a perfect pearl that will command a great price, so he sells all that he has to acquire it. In God's eyes, you are that pearl of great price. The Word of God emptied himself and became a man. He sacrificed everything to purchase your freedom and claim you for himself. Jesus Christ paid the ultimate price on the cross so that you would never doubt how much you are loved. On the evening of the Last Supper, he said to the apostles, "No one has greater love than this, to lay down one's life for one's friends" (Jn 15:13).

As if this great act of love on the cross was not enough, Jesus tells us directly how much we are worth in God's eyes when he tells us that we have nothing to fear or worry about because the Father in heaven watches over each and every one of our needs:

> Notice the ravens: they do not sow or reap; they have neither storehouse nor barn, yet God feeds them. How much more important are you than birds! . . . Notice how the flowers grow. They do not toil or spin. But I tell you, not even Solomon in all his splendor was dressed like one of them (Lk 12: 24, 27).

The Source of Our Dignity

The modern world has a skewed view of what gives a person dignity. We tend to think that our dignity is tied up in our possessions, our status, our accomplishments, or our position in society. But none of these things is powerful enough or stable enough to convey the innate dignity that each of us has in the eyes of God.

A friend of mine is caring for his elderly father. His father can do little for himself. He is weak and sickly, and it is difficult for him to get out of bed. But my friend loves his father. He visits him daily in the nursing facility. He brings his father little treats and tokens of his affection. He tells the staff stories of his father's younger days, the adventures he had as a young man and the kind of father he was. My friend's love for his father shines out. Thanks to my friend's dedication, the staff treat my friend's father with a little extra respect. They don't know him. They don't have any reason to consider him in any different light than any of the other patients in the nursing home. So why do they take a little extra time with him and speak to him more gently? Because he is loved.

A baby can't do anything for herself. She can't bathe or feed or dress herself. She can't help pay the bills or clean the house. Despite all this, strangers see her and say how beautiful and precious she is. Why? Because she is loved.

Our dignity and value as persons do not derive from what we can do. They are anchored in God's undying, perpetual love for us. As the quote at the beginning of this chapter asserts, each person is sacred and worthy of awe because of God's miraculous love for us. Even if the love of others fails, God's love never fails (see 1 Chr 16:34). God loves you so much that not only has he made you in his image, but he was born, lived, suffered, died, and rose again so that you might know how much you are worth to him. And if that wasn't enough, he loves you so much that he wants to make you a god—a being who is perfect and immortal and intimately united to himself—so that you can spend all of eternity being loved by him.

The Root of Our Longing for Dignity

St. John Paul the Great has asserted that in the beginning, before the Fall, we experienced an "Original Unity" where we were intimately aware of God's love for us (2006). We were made to be loved and to be aware of how much God loves us. That love enabled us to stand "naked and not ashamed" (Gn 2:25) in the eyes of God. That is to say, confident in God's undying love for us and the innate dignity that love has bestowed on us, we had no doubts about our worth or the value of any other human person. We had nothing to fear and nothing of which to be ashamed on any level of our physical, psychological, emotional, or spiritual being.

Then sin entered the world, and with it came shame. What is the first thing Adam and Eve do after they eat the forbidden fruit of the Garden? They hear God taking his daily stroll through Eden, and they hide themselves.

> When they heard the sound of the LORD God walking about in the garden at the breezy time of the day, the man and his wife hid themselves from the LORD God among the trees of the garden. The LORD God then called to the man and asked him: Where are you? He answered, "I heard you in the garden; but I was afraid, because I was naked, so I hid" (Gn 3:8-10).

St. John Paul the Great argues that their hiding themselves indicates that when sin (the choosing of our own path as opposed to God's plan for our fulfillment) entered the world, we separated ourselves from God and experienced the fear and shame that comes from being separate, exposed, vulnerable. We feel ashamed at how little we are, how insufficient we are, without God. We were naked all along, but we were covered by God's grace. Having ripped away that cloak of grace, we are exposed to spiritual elements in a way that leaves us feeling powerless, terrified, nowhere near up to the task before us—what Sartre referred to as existential nausea. What chance does a few ounces of carbon and water stand against the enormity of the universe? We must remember that *our dignity comes from sharing in God's divinity, which is our destiny*. Having separated ourselves from that path, we realize how little we are on our own, and for the first time, we feel a lack, we feel small, insufficient, and utterly undignified.

But dignity is both our original state and our ultimate destiny. Although we lost it, we still remember it. Our need for it tugs at our souls, and we ache for its restoration. This ache has continued to be felt through the ages as the divine longing for dignity. We all know that we are worth more than . . . *this*. That is, we intuit, somehow, that we were meant to be more than whatever it is we are now. No matter how much or how little we have accomplished, we recognize that it is nothing compared to what we are meant to be and do. As Qoheleth remarked, "Vanity of vanities, all things are vanity" (Eccl 1:2)!

We were once united to God, and his intimate presence warmed us. We were covered by his protection; he made us his sons and daughters, marked us as his own, and confirmed in us the sense that with him we were capable of anything. But having lost all of this, we desperately grasp for anything that will give us some vague sense of worth or meaning— however fleeting. We know intuitively that we cannot restore our divine dignity by our own power, so we seek to prove our worth in the only pathetic manner we think is available to us: trying to be superior to—or at least "as good as"—others. This is the sin of envy.

How Envy Distorts the Longing for Dignity

Envy makes life a competition that we either are always in danger of losing or have already lost. Envy whispers in our spiritual ears that if we could only have X we could be worthwhile, we could be complete, we could be "as good as" the next person. The problem with this is that even if we could be "as good as" our neighbor, our brother, our co-worker, or the person in the pew down from us, we still would not be the gods we were meant to become. That is why enough is never enough. Our longing for dignity can be fulfilled only by pursuing the divinity that is our destiny. Envy causes us to confuse this ache for divinity with a desire for things that pass away. Wanting to acquire the good things this world has to offer is not bad. The sin of envy is not really about wanting things. We should never feel guilty for wanting to enjoy the good things God has made in this world. As the Yiddish proverb says, "God will hold us accountable for failing to enjoy all the pleasures he has permitted." Or, as St. John Bosco put it, "Enjoy yourself as much as you like—if only you keep from sin."

Envy is a sin because it means pretending that the pursuit of the things of this world is sufficient to satisfy our deeper longing for divinity. Remember that sinning means "accepting less than what God wants to give us." Trying to backfill the void in our souls with acquisitions and accomplishments never satisfies, not because we are bad people who are naturally grasping and greedy, or because the things of this world that we pine for are necessarily bad, but rather because, at the deepest level of our being, we intuit that this is not what we truly long for.

Of course, we don't just envy the material and temporal

things we see in the store or peek at through our neighbor's windows. Sometimes the things that drive our envy can seem quite good and even noble.

"If I have to go to one more bridal shower, I think I'm going to vomit," Charlotte said. Charlotte's fiancé broke up with her six months ago for another girl.

"It's getting to the point that I dread going to the mailbox. Every time I do, it seems like another friend is sending me a shower announcement or a "save the date!" I want to be happy for them, but I can't. I can't stand to be around them, look at their rings, listen to them chatter about their wedding plans. I'm embarrassed to admit it, but sometimes I have a hard time even turning on the TV. Seeing an engagement ring commercial can wreck my entire day. I just want to crawl into a hole. I'm so angry at God. It's one thing to take away my dream, but does God have to rub my face in it?"

There are no easy answers for the kind of very real and very deep pain that Charlotte feels, but if she isn't careful, the envy she is struggling with will only force her deeper and deeper into the darkness of her pain, where no grace can reach her and no hope can be found.

The Social Dimension of Envy

The Thomson's gazelle is the McDonald's Big Mac of the Serengeti. Every predator eats them. But because they are herd animals, they are not so easily taken. They are fast, and they have powerful antlers they can use to attack or defend themselves with. If a lioness wants to stop and pick up some fast food for her cubs, she knows that she needs to separate her prey from the herd. A single gazelle is relatively easy pickings.

Social envy is a tool that Satan uses to ensnare us. Humans are social animals. Our communal nature is an essential part of our humanity. Stress is always hard, and remaining faithful under stress is always harder still, but if our supportive relationships remain intact, we can usually rally. Satan knows this, so he uses his best tricks to get us alone. Where pride causes us to stand alone, convincing us that we have no need of others, envy causes us to stand at a distance from those who could support us. God wants us to remain safe and in close communion with him, yet Satan wants us to stand apart so that he can devour us. Envy makes us despise the company of others. Envy causes us to look at all the blessings God has given others and, instead of being inspired to hope that God's generosity will be similarly manifested, in some way, in our own lives, envy brings us the despair of thinking that we must be worth nothing because we do not have everything those around us have.

The Antidote: The Heavenly Virtue of Kindness

Traditionally, the heavenly virtue of kindness has been promoted as the antidote to envy, but few people really understand why. If envy is a distortion of the divine longing for dignity, kindness gives us the ability to both locate and rediscover the center of our dignity. Kindness is one of the fruits of the spirit (Gal 5:22-23). In other words, it is one of the qualities that shine out of us when we are connected to God's love for us. Remember, our dignity is rooted in the fact that God loves us. Likewise, we remind others of their dignity by loving them. Those same people remind us of our dignity by loving us back. The Greek word for kindness is *chrestotes,* which means "benignity, tender concern, and uprightness."

Classically, love is universally understood by theologians, philosophers, and psychologists as the commitment to will and work for the good of the other. Kindness might properly be considered to be love's little sister. Kindness is the commitment to look for little ways we can work for the good of others, to use what we have to make another's day easier or more pleasant through simple acts of generosity. Through those simple acts of kindness, we reverse all the ways that envy undermines our dignity. To be kind, we must first reconnect to our sense of God's love for us, which reminds us of our dignity. That connection leads us to want to restore connection with others, to promote their dignity, by looking for simple ways to care for them. The more we commit ourselves to making simple acts of kindness, the more *we enable others to flourish just by being in our presence.*

Think about that last sentence for a moment. What would it be like to be the sort of person who enables others to flourish just by walking into the room? That strikes me as a particularly awesome superpower. Pope Francis appears to have this superpower in spades. When he was first elected to the papacy, public perception of the Catholic Church was, understandably, at an all-time low. Within a year of his election, the world was willing to give Catholicism another hearing primarily because of simple but powerful acts of kindness such as cold-calling a woman who was pregnant out of wedlock and promising to baptize her baby personally; embracing a man covered in disfiguring tumors due to neurofibromatosis; letting an autistic child play on the stage while he addressed an international audience for the Pontifical Council for the Family; and giving yet another child a ride in the Popemobile. Simple gestures such as these and others like them have communicated not only the pope's genuine warmth, but also his deep regard for the dignity of others, and that, in turn, affirmed the dignity of the pope and the church he represents.

Brain scientist Dr. Daniel Siegel notes that "kindness is integration made visible" (2012). Siegel's research employing functional brain imaging shows that kindness is the sign of the brain working at its best. The kind brain, as it were, shows better cross-communication between the left and right hemispheres and the higher (cortex) and lower (limbic) brain, which allows a person to exhibit higher levels of insight, mindfulness, and self-control. When the human brain is optimally doing its job of integrating input from your body, thoughts, and relationships, you feel a sense of harmony within yourself and your relationships. This harmony is most often expressed both as kindness toward oneself (evidenced by being forgiving of one's mistakes and attending thoughtfully to one's physical, emotional, and spiritual needs) and kindness to others (evidenced by making simple gestures that communicate how one cherishes another). Siegel notes that from a brain-based perspective, kindness is one of the best indicators that we are functioning at our best as biological, psychological, and relational persons. Further, kindness is not just a sign of a well-functioning person; being kind can actually help restore the brain to a state of regulation from a state of dysregulation. Depressed or anxious persons who intentionally focus on simple ways they might be kind to others not only lift their subjective moods but end up with healthier functioning brains (Layous, Chancellor, Lyubomirsky, et al., 2011). Being intentionally kind actually helps the brain reset itself after stress; it restores us to a state of improved body, mind, and relational integration.

The Kindness Connection

Besides being good for us, kindness is a powerful way of affirming the dignity of others. Years ago when I was walking in downtown Pittsburgh with a friend, we came upon a homeless person who was sitting in a doorway of an abandoned storefront. My friend and I both gave the man a few dollars, but my friend looked at the man and said, "Here you go, man. What's your name?"

The homeless man looked a little stunned. He wasn't sure he had heard right. My friend asked him again, "What's your name?"

"Jack."

My friend held out his hand to shake Jack's hand. "Good to meet you, Jack. I'm Michael. You here often?"

"Yep. Every day."

"You like coffee?"

"Sure."

"How do you like your coffee?"

"I like it sweet!"

"Well, I'll tell you what, Jack. Next time I come this way, I'll bring you a cup of black coffee with some extra sugar, okay?"

"Okay. Cream too?"

"You got it. Cream and extra sugar. You take care of yourself. I'll see you next time."

"God bless you."

"Thank you, Jack! God bless you too, man."

The whole exchange lasted maybe thirty seconds, but what a powerful witness my friend was to me. He didn't just chuck a few dollars at a homeless man as he continued on talking to me about more interesting things. He took a minute to care about the person sitting there at his feet, find out his name, and learn something about him. It was a completely unremarkable conversation that, to me, was a remarkable act of kindness. It didn't just make me see Jack in a different light; it made me see my friend in a different light too. In that moment, I saw both Jack's dignity and my friend's in a new light. It was a simple but transcendent moment that elevated all of us.

Being kind helps us rediscover where our true dignity is located, namely, in reminding ourselves that God loves us and then communicating that love to others.

When we are suffering from envy, we can decrease the pain and at the same time fulfill our divine longing for dignity by rising above ourselves and being kind to someone else.

Annie describes herself as a reluctant stay-at-home mom. She lost her job as the marketing VP at an ad agency about a year ago and hasn't been able to find a suitable position since. Her husband, Tom, was happy that Annie decided to stay home and felt that she was contributing to the household finances by saving on childcare and other work-related expenses. Annie agreed that there were real benefits to a parent being home, but she often felt like she was going a little stir-crazy as the days dragged on with her children Bethany (age four) and John (two).

"I love my kids, and I feel like an awful person for saying this, but I was so jealous that Tom got to go to work every day," Annie says. "I was jealous that he got to go to lunch with his co-workers. I was jealous that he got to feel like he was accomplishing something. I was jealous that he brought home a paycheck because I believed it made what he did matter more than what I did. I was jealous of the whole thing. I knew he wasn't out partying all day, but I just craved the adult interaction and really missed using my business degree. Sometimes I felt like my brain was rotting.

"I found myself becoming truly resentful of the whole situation. I felt like a failure for losing my job in the first place, and I suppose I started letting the whole thing eat at me. I would plop the kids in front of a video and be on Facebook chatting with people. I would snap at Tom when he came home. I wasn't doing well at all.

"I let my prayer life go too. I was angry with God for taking away my job and forcing me to come home. But one night I started to pray again. I'm not really sure why. I don't remember feeling a whole lot different at the time, but afterward I felt guilty for letting myself get to this place. I knew something had to change inside me. I knew a lot of women would kill to trade places with me. I could at least try to appreciate the opportunity to be home—at least until I could find a position that would suit me and our family.

"I worked on trying to be kinder to the kids throughout the day. I'd try to enter into their games instead of being irritated while they played around me. I would do my best to look into their eyes when they were talking to me or sit on the floor and invite them to sit on my lap when they wanted to show me something. I tried to make more of the things Tom liked to eat and save some energy to talk and just hang out with him instead of tagging him with the kids the second he came in the door so I could go for a walk or get a bath.

"At first, I could feel myself really fighting back against it. I wasn't about to become some fifties TV mom. But I just kept trying to be me, just kinder. I read something on a mommy blog that really hit me. It said, 'The parents' job is to reflect the love of God to our kids.' That really struck me. I hadn't thought of it that way before. I kept going with it all, and I guess I was actually surprised when I started feeling a change. I felt like I was getting in touch with the dignity of this new role I had taken on. I'm in a really different place. I would still like to return to work, but I'm beginning to get what some women see in being home with their kids. The other day, Bethany and John and I were laughing so hard over an art project we were doing. I just caught myself thinking that I wouldn't want to miss this for the world. I had to laugh because it was almost like I had forgotten I was supposed to be resentful. I enjoyed my job, and, like I said, I'm not ready to say I'd never go back, but I'm starting to see that my dignity isn't tied up in the position. My dignity is tied up in how much God loves me and how well I show his love to my family. I think that's pretty cool now that I'm in a much better place with the whole thing."

Annie discovered another of Pope Francis's secrets. He once encouraged parents to "waste time with your children" (Wooden, 2013). The pope understands that one of the best ways to be kind to someone—especially our children—is to waste time with them. Just being there with someone as if you had nowhere else to go and nowhere else to be—even if it's only for five minutes at a time.

Kindness roots us. It anchors our dignity in things that matter and reminds us that our destiny is to become a more effective conduit of God's love. Being kind facilitates our divinization by allowing us to have a taste of the joy God feels when he makes all of creation come alive and flourish in his presence. The heavenly virtue of kindness quenches the divine thirst for dignity by reminding us that our dignity comes from our ability to reflect his transformative power in even the smallest moments of everyday life.

Satisfying the Divine Longing for Dignity: An Exercise

PRAY

Lord Jesus Christ,

It is so hard for me to see others enjoying the things that I want. I pray, Lord, that you will satisfy all the desires of my heart and help me to be open to the ways you would like to fulfill my deepest longings. While I wait, help me to practice kindness. Help me to pull out of my own pain, frustration, and bitterness and actively look for the simple ways I can be a blessing to others. Help me to know that my dignity is not won or lost by achieving things but from being loved by you and sharing that love with others. In Jesus's name. Amen.

COAL: Fuel for Change

As you consider ways to better satisfy your divine longing for dignity, take a moment to think about how COAL might be your fuel for change.

CURIOSITY AND OPENNESS

Ask yourself: Where did I learn that my worth depended upon keeping up with those around me?

Who taught me to think this way about myself?

What situations impressed this lesson on me?

Do I want to continue to allow these experiences to rule my life?

Do not judge or edit yourself. Receive your answers in a spirit of openness and grace.

ACCEPTANCE

Say, "These are the experiences that have shaped my struggle to satisfy my divine longing for dignity. I accept my past even as I accept God's call to change and grow."

LOVE

Loving myself means working to become the person God wants me to be. I know that I can fulfill my deepest longing for dignity only by being kind to those around me, especially those who may be better off than I am.

Ask yourself: In those times when I feel jealous or resentful, what would it look like to display kindness where I currently exhibit envy?

> What obstacles would I have to overcome to achieve this goal?

> What help, resources, or support might I need to overcome these obstacles?

> Say, "I will love myself and accept God's love for me by choosing this path of kindness over the temptation to envy."

Review these loving resolutions each morning. Imagine a time in the coming day when you might be tempted to envy. Imagine responding instead with kindness. Ask for God's help to remember this more loving response in those times when you are being tempted to give in to those jealous impulses.

Practicing Kindness: Action Items

If you are struggling with envy and would like to discover how you can begin to satisfy your divine longing for dignity, consider the following questions:

> Think of a time when someone was particularly kind to you. How did it make you feel? What could you do this week to make someone feel similarly cherished by you?

> Make a list of twenty-five simple things you could do to make the lives of those around you easier or more pleasant.

The Divine Longing for Dignity: A Promise

God wants you to know how much you are worth, not because of what you have or what you have accomplished, but simply because he loves you. On those days when you feel like you are not enough, or that you will never be enough, know that none of that matters. Resist the envy you feel with all your heart and call out to God. Ask him to help you see yourself through his eyes. Breathe in his love. Rest in that love. Then celebrate the fact that you are loved more than all the stars in the universe, more than all the birds of the air and the flowers of the field, by sharing that love through a small act of kindness performed for someone who needs a similar reminder of their true worth. Be the person who inspires others to flourish just by being in your presence.

Chapter Six

Satisfying the Divine Longing for Justice

The time is out of joint.
O, cursed spite,
that ever I was born to set it right!
—*Hamlet, Act 1, scene 5, lines 190-191*

Life is no picnic. Turning on the news is almost always a terrifying experience. And on the personal front, it can be hard to get through the first few hours of the morning without being affronted by some injustice, no matter how petty. The kids left their toys on the stairs, again. Your spouse slept in and now is being irritable with you as he or she runs around trying to get ready for work. Maybe you're still fuming about the comment your sister made over the weekend. No, things are not the way things are supposed to be.

Frankly, it has always seemed curious to me that we expect things should be different and somehow *better* than they are. On what, exactly, do we realistically base this expectation? Perfection is completely outside of our experience. When have we *ever* encountered everything literally going exactly as it should? On those rare days when even *most* things go according to plan, doesn't it seem like something just short of a miracle? *Chaos is the norm*, yet we never seem to expect it. No matter how normal, even natural, *dis*order is, we never count on it as reason says we should. Contrary to conventional wisdom, with so much imperfection, chaos, and, yes, evil filling our days, isn't it strange that we should simply assume that the world should *work* better than it does? Where does this strange and incredible presumption come from?

The Root of Our Longing

In his Sermon on the Mount, Jesus tells us that those who hunger and thirst for justice will be blessed (Mt 5:6). "Justice" refers to the work of making things as they should be, as God intends them to be, in our lives, our relationships, and the world at large. As the *Catechism of the Catholic Church* puts it,

> Justice is the moral virtue that consists in the constant and firm will to give their due to God and neighbor. Justice toward God is called the "virtue of religion." Justice toward men disposes one to respect the rights of each and to establish in human relationships the harmony that promotes equity with regard to persons and to the common good (*CCC*, no. 1807).

In short, justice is the right order that exists between people and the world when everything and everyone is given their due and behaves as they ought. Like all the divine longings, our divine longing for justice—the foundation for our natural *expectation* that everything should work infinitely better than it does—was given to us at the dawn of creation. Recall that Original Unity is the state of being that existed between God and Adam and Eve before the Fall. In that time, St. John Paul the Great reminds us (with apologies to Douglas Adams), *life, the universe, and everything* were in perfect order. There was complete harmony between God and his creation. Life was *just*.

After the Fall, things became decidedly unjust. Righteousness was disrupted. Nature was unhooked from grace. Men and women were at odds (Gn 3:12-14). People turned radically against each other (Gn 4:8). Nation turned against nation (Gn 11:1-10). *Even the earth* fought our efforts to till the soil (see Gn 3:17).

But despite the fact that we have grown used to everything rebelling against us, somewhere deep inside we remember that we once had more. We once had order. We once had peace. *We once had justice.* Despite knowing that everything is hopelessly out of whack, we long for the return to the harmony that existed when God, humankind, and the world were at peace with one another.

The Great Injustice

The loss of this harmony is the Great Injustice that still has humanity reeling today. This pain exacerbates every other injustice we experience—big or small—during our earthly life. Imagine that I suffered a football injury in my shoulder when I was young, and twenty years later, on a rainy day, you bump into that shoulder while passing me in the hallway. I wince in pain. Perhaps it would have been uncomfortable to have you bump into me even if I hadn't been injured before, but I experience my present pain all the more acutely because of the old injury. The same is true for the pain we feel over frustrated expectations, big and small offenses, and other injustices. Every pain is made worse by the distance that exists in the relationship between the injured person and God.

Though most of us don't recognize it, each of us has a deep pool of angst just below the surface. All it takes is some un-expected personal wound to rip off the scab before we start raging. It isn't because the traffic made us late for the meet-ing. It is because, underneath it all, the deepest parts of our humanity feel naked without God, and the powerlessness of feeling totally, utterly, terrifyingly alone is mind-numbingly infuriating.

But it is not the pain of the present that is the problem. It is our distance from God that is the true source of our impo-tent rage. The spiritual traveler who is walking the *illuminative* or the *unitive* way will offer a profoundly different and more patient response to even the most hurtful offenses than will the person who has not yet begun to walk even the *purgative* way. That's because the latter is farther away from God and has not yet learned to surrender and tap into the graces that God can provide. Our ability to practice the spiritual work of mercy that is "bearing wrongs patiently" is greatly impacted by where we find ourselves on the path of divinization. Why? Because as we experience the progressive healing of the deeper injustice caused by separation from God, we find we have more resources available to contend with the lesser sufferings of this world. Embracing the call to divinization facilitates the satisfaction of our divine longing for justice—restoration of our union with God—thereby enabling us to have a more responsibly engaged (as opposed to a reactively impulsive) atti-tude toward the injustices we experience in the here and now.

In that here and now, the divine longing for justice com-pels us to challenge the injustice we encounter in life, and work to build God's kingdom however we can. God's plan of divinization means setting not just us but the entire universe right again. One day we will be a new creation and we will see the new heaven and the new earth (Rv 21:1), where, once again, harmony between us and others will be restored to a degree that is unimaginable in our post-fallen state. In the meantime, our divine longing for justice propels us to seek out and create this harmony where we can. The longing for justice does not simply remind us of what was lost to us; it reminds us of God's intention to make things right again. It challenges us in the here and now to cooperate with his grace to do what we can to create harmony with other people and in the world.

Wrath: The Distortion of the Divine Longing for Justice

Many Christians believe that wrath is the simple act of getting angry at an offense or injustice. In my counseling practice, I encounter many people who have been hurt deeply by others—people who carry deep wounds from abusive parents, philandering spouses, unjust bosses and co-workers, spiteful family members and frenemies, and more. But while many of my clients remain deeply angry at the profound hurt they have experienced at the hands of others, they often feel terribly guilty about being angry, and they wonder if they are committing some sort of sin. As one client put it, "I can forgive, but I can't forget, and when I remember what my parents did to me, the anger just floods me."

But anger itself isn't sinful. How can it be? God created it just like he created all of our emotions, and God pronounced all that he created as "good" (see Gn 1:31). Anger is a product of the same neuroendocrine system that is responsible for our hunger and reproductive drives. Properly ordered, anger is nothing more than the emotional response to an injustice. It is the warning light on the human dashboard that grabs our attention and says, "This is not the way things are supposed to be!"

Anger itself is not a problem. It is how we respond to anger that can be either righteous or problematic. If we allow our anger to motivate us to take *thoughtful, appropriate, respectful,* and *proportionate* action to correct an injustice, right a wrong, or restore harmonious order, our anger can be said to be righteous, even godly! But those four words—*thoughtful, appropriate, respectful,* and *proportionate*—are the keys to determining whether our anger is just and righteous or whether it is an indulgence of the deadly sin of wrath. Whereas anger motivates us to do what we reasonably and respectfully can to make things right, wrath causes us to act in a manner that inevitably makes things much, much worse. Wrath is anger that is expressed in a manner that is *rash, inappropriate, disrespectful,* and *disproportionate*.

Bill crushed his wife's heart when he cheated on her with Britta, a woman he met at the gym. When his wife, Margie, confronted him, he broke down in tears and said that he had been trying to end the relationship, but Britta had threatened to tell Margie everything. He called Britta that day and told her it was over. He canceled his gym membership. He also changed his cell phone number. Bill asked Margie to go to counseling with him. They went for a couple of sessions, but ultimately Margie quit going. It was just too painful. Although it has been months since the affair was over, Margie still has a hard time being in the same room with Bill. When he talks to her, the discussion inevitably circles back around to the infidelity. Every petty irritation becomes "just another reason I can't trust you."

Bill has reached out to their pastor for support. He has tried to encourage Margie to forgive him and surrender her anger, but she denies that she's angry. She says, "I don't have a problem. Bill is the one who cheated. I'm not even angry anymore. I've forgiven him, but I'll never forget what he did. I don't think it would be reasonable to suggest that I should. I'm not going to divorce him. But I will never let him into my heart again."

Although Margie's behavior is unfortunate, it's important to remember the longing for justice that is at the root of her actions. All she wanted was for Bill to understand how deeply she was hurt. Unfortunately, the path she chose in her quest for justice simply locked the whole family in an ever-widening spiral of pain. Margie had a right to demand justice for the offenses that her husband committed against her. But what she was doing to her husband couldn't help but make things infinitely worse. As St. Ambrose once wisely said, "No one heals himself by wounding another."

Ambrose's observation nicely illustrates the insidious nature of wrath. It turns our anger into an arrow we can shoot right into the heart of the person we believe has wronged us. It can feel so good sometimes, but it ends up dragging us down, demeaning us, alienating the very people from whom we want real justice. More to the point, when we are in the clutches of wrath, we are convinced that we can be satisfied by the justice we can achieve for ourselves in this life, but that's simply not true. For every offense we heal, there will be another offense waiting around the corner to disturb our peace. That may strike some people as a depressing thought, but it's depressing only if you believe that our divine longing for justice can be completely sated by pursuing worldly justice exclusively. To find true satisfaction, of course we must pursue justice in this world, but we must pursue that justice in a manner that simultaneously addresses the deeper wound caused by the Fall and the loss of Original Unity and is consistent with our call to divinization.

The Heavenly Virtue Patience: Antidote to Wrath

Satisfying our divine longing for justice requires us to practice the heavenly virtue of patience. Many believe that being patient means putting up with offensive people and just "letting things go." But there is a big difference between patience and indulgence.

Being patient enables us to make a *thoughtful, appropriate, respectful,* and *proportionate* response to an injustice. It enables me to step back from the injury, assess what's really going on, and ascertain what I might be able to do to actually fix it. Patience gives me the space to let responsible attempts to address an injustice mature. It helps me maintain a peaceful spirit while I address the offenses committed against me, not because I don't care how things turn out, but because I know that by cooperating with God's grace, I can be confident that my efforts will pay off either in the form of an actual resolution to the problem or at least in some measures that can bring relief while I continue working on the larger issue. Finally, when I practice patience, I allow my responses to earthly injustices to simultaneously heal, in small ways, the Great Injustice that is my ongoing separation from

God. Practicing this kind of intentional, mindful patience (as opposed to mindless resignation) propels me to seek shelter under God's wings (Ps 17:8), to allow my heart to soften in the warmth of his care, to become more pliable in his hands.

Patience isn't just good for the soul. It blesses every part of our lives. Psychologists refer to the virtue of patience as "delayed gratification," the willingness to forgo smaller, short-term gains so that a larger, long-term gain might be acquired. For instance, I could spend what's left of my paycheck after bills on a weekend in Las Vegas, or I could save what's left for my kid's college fund, or my dream home, or an even nicer trip. Decades of research shows that the ability to be patient—that is, to delay gratification—directly correlates with the amount of life and relationship satisfaction a person can expect from his or her life. In the famous Stanford marshmallow experiment of the early 1970s, four-year-olds were told they could eat a marshmallow now or wait fifteen minutes and have two marshmallows. Subsequent studies done on the test subjects demonstrated that the children who were able to wait for the second marshmallow were ten years later considered to be more competent by parents and teachers, and twenty years later they scored an average of 210 points higher on the SAT. Our capacity for patience has tremendous influence on our overall health, wealth, and well-being.

Patience ultimately facilitates our divinization by reminding us of the higher goal that we are pursuing every moment. Patience helps us to attend to both the immediate and the ancient wounds in our hearts and souls; it enables us to take the time we need to cultivate a godly plan of action.

Carl often felt attacked, criticized, and put down even when others swore that they didn't mean to hurt him. He was quick to shut down any interaction that even seemed like it would be potentially hurtful.

"As far as I was concerned, it didn't matter whether they meant to hurt me or not," Carl said. "I'd been through enough garbage in my life. I didn't need to take any more from people no matter where it came from or why it happened."

His quick temper was especially hard on his wife and children. When his wife let him down in some small way, or if she dared to express a disappointment in even the gentlest manner, he would quickly go on the offensive. He was unwilling to brook any resistance or hesitation on his children's part if he asked them to do something. He expected them to do it immediately. It was this expectation that finally forced a change.

"I was working on a project, and my son, Ben, walked in," Carl remembered. "I asked him to get a tool for me. He said that he couldn't, and I stopped him cold. I shouted at him and told him that I wasn't putting up with his laziness or disrespect and that he better get his ass in gear. He started to cry, and I told him if he didn't stop, I'd give him something to cry about."

Carl's wife, Sandee, heard the exchange and rushed into the room, her hands and face covered in blood. She had a terrible nosebleed and asked Ben to run and get her some paper towels to stanch the bleeding so that she could clean herself up. She called Carl a bully and told him that if he didn't learn to get control of himself, he'd have to leave.

"She was standing there, bleeding all over the place, screaming at me, and all I could think was, 'What have I done?'" Carl said.

Carl called a counselor that day and started working on dealing more effectively with anger. "I learned that I didn't have to just ride the wave of my feelings," he said. "I always thought that if I felt angry, I didn't have a choice but to go with it. But my counselor helped me realize that just like a wave, anger peaks and then crashes. If you can wait to respond until the wave collapses on itself, you'll feel more in control and be able to respond in a more thoughtful, respectful way.

"Now, when I feel my anger building, I just close my eyes and imagine the wave. I try to breathe through it. Once it rolls in to shore, I ask myself if there's anything I need to do to solve the problem or if this is something I just need to let go of. I'm able to let a lot more things go than I ever used to, and I feel okay about it. When I can't let something go, I'm able to address it in a way that gets other people to actually listen to me. I'll always feel sad about the time I lost to my anger, but I'm grateful that I'm learning to be more patient. It really *is* helping me be a better man."

Carl and Sandee describe a fairly common domestic situation where wrath can have a powerful negative impact and patience can bring profound healing. In the beginning of his story, Carl describes one of the chief confusions among people who struggle with the sin of wrath, namely, they believe that their only alternative to acting out their anger is stuffing their rage. Many Christians believe that this is how they are meant to deal with their anger, but this is unacceptable. In his *Book of Pastoral Rule*, St. Gregory the Great counsels: "Anger seethes all the more when corralled by the violent guard of an indiscreet silence."

As St. Gregory the Great observes, patience does not require us to stuff our emotions; instead it gives us a chance to breathe in the calming breath of God so that, infused with grace, our anger might become a medicine that treats the wound of injustice rather than a poison that spreads it.

But if this is true in such common situations as the domestic drama between Carl and Sandee, what about more serious situations? How do the temptation to wrath and the virtue of patience play out in situations where there is a long-standing injustice?

Cecilia recalls a childhood filled with humiliating punishments, cruel comments, mocking, resentful uninterest, and often painful physical injuries inflicted in the name of discipline. Worse, her parents were very well regarded in their community and in the parish in which she grew up. In his later years, Cecilia's father was ordained a deacon. In addition to enduring the abuse, she regularly had to hear people tell her about how wonderful her parents were. "It made me sick," Cecilia said.

Understandably, she had little to do with her parents as an adult. Years of counseling, spiritual direction, and eventually a loving, supportive marriage to Frank allowed her to heal many of her childhood wounds, although she still struggled with some feelings of insecurity and poor self-worth.

Over the years, as she healed, Cecilia allowed herself to have limited contact with her parents. Christmas cards. A phone call. Dinner in a public place. "They could never admit what they did to me, though," she said. "When I tried to bring it up, they either denied it or turned things around on me somehow. There were times when the anger inside me welled up so much that I wished them dead."

In time, Cecilia's mother died, and her father, who was the crueler parent, was diagnosed with colon cancer. "At first I was surprised at how glad I was. I wanted him to know how it felt to be afraid and alone and vulnerable and to have the very people who were supposed to care turn their backs on you. By then, though, I was in a really different place. I had spent years working through the mess they had left inside of me. God's love had really taken hold in my life and I knew what I was worth. I didn't need my father to affirm me or validate what I knew to be true. People tell me that they would have just written off my parents if they were like mine, that they admire my patience, but a lot of the time I didn't feel very patient.

"When my dad got cancer, I wanted to have as little to do with him as I could. He was financially well off enough that I could have just put him somewhere and let him live out his last miserable days. But I knew that God wanted more from me. I couldn't bring him home, that just couldn't have worked, but I made it a point to spend an hour a day with him. What a penance that was at first. I practically itched to get out of the room the entire time I was there. But as time went by, something started to change between us. He never admitted what he had done to me, but he would sometimes tell me about his own childhood. I never knew a lot about my grandfather. I knew he was a bad guy, but I never really understood how bad. It turns out he died in jail. He was a violent alcoholic, and he took out his anger on my grandmother and their eight kids. One day he got in a bar fight with some guy. My grandfather punched him and the guy fell backward on a broken beer bottle that pierced his lung. The man died, and that was the last my father ever saw of his old man. He was twelve at the time.

"He had to quit school and work to help pay the bills. He was out on his own by the time he was sixteen. I knew he had a hard life, but by the time I came along he was a successful businessman. I never really knew the details, and I never really cared to know. Anyway, it isn't like any of that made up for what he had done to me, but at the same time I guess I saw how much better he had done than his father had. I used to think of my father as this complete evil bastard who really didn't care how much he hurt me. Listening to him, I guess I saw that he really had tried to do better by me. He could never say he was sorry, but he wanted me to know in his own backward way that he had tried to do better.

"I was there when he died. It was a peaceful death. Part of me, even at the end, felt like it was more than he deserved. But a bigger part of me was glad that he didn't suffer more than he did. And I was glad that I took the time to work things out between us as much as I did.

"Through it all, I felt God doing some really powerful stuff in my heart. It's hard to put it into words, but it would be so exhausting going in there sometimes, I would usually spend a few minutes in the chapel before I went in to see him. Something about spending that time with my heavenly Father reminded me that I was safe, and I that didn't have to be afraid to see my biological father. I'm still sorting it all out, but I know that the whole experience was very healing for me. Not at all the way I expected, but I grew on a lot of levels through the whole thing. And I'm grateful that God gave me the chance to grow closer to him through it all. I don't know if my dad's in heaven or not. But at least now I can pray that he is, and maybe, even, I'll be glad to see him again someday."

Cecilia's story is dramatic, but her example illustrates the different levels of healing that God wants to facilitate in the hearts of those who patiently address the wounds their anger points toward. Whether or not your own story contains pain that deep, taking the time you need to practice patience in the face of your anger can help you to respond to your hurts—present, past, and existential—in a way that truly satisfies the divine longing for justice.

Satisfying the Divine Longing for Justice: An Exercise

PRAY

Lord Jesus Christ,

You said, "Blessed are they who hunger and thirst for justice." Bless me, Lord. Give me patience that I might respond gracefully to the slights and offenses I encounter in my life. Allow my efforts to restore justice to bear mature fruit. Grant me the justice I seek, Lord, but remind me to always seek justice in just ways that I might not simply heal the hurt, but bring healing to the broken Body of Christ. I ask all of this in the Name of Jesus Christ, whom I claim as the Lord of my longing for justice. Amen.

COAL: Fuel for Change

As you consider ways that you could better respond to your divine longing for justice, take a moment to consider how COAL can be your fuel for change.

CURIOSITY AND OPENNESS
Ask yourself: Where did I learn that the best way to respond to injuries was to lash out?

> Who taught me this response?
>
> What situations impressed this lesson on me?
>
> Do I want to continue to allow these experiences to rule my life?

Do not judge or edit yourself. Receive your answers in a spirit of openness and grace.

ACCEPTANCE
Say, "These are the experiences that have shaped my struggle to satisfy my divine longing for justice. I accept my past even as I accept God's call for me to change and grow."

LOVE
Loving myself means working to become the person God wants me to be. I know that I can fulfill my deep-

est longing for justice only by responding with patience to the offenses and struggles I face.

> In those times when I feel hurt and angry, what would it look like to display patience where I currently exhibit wrath?

> What obstacles would I have to overcome to achieve this goal?

> What help, resources, or support might I need to overcome these obstacles?

> Say, "I will love myself and accept God's love for me by choosing this path of patience over giving in to the temptation to wrath."

Review these loving resolutions each morning. Imagine a time in the coming day when you might be tempted to wrath. Imagine responding instead with patience. Ask for God's help to remember this more loving response in those times when your patience is tested.

Practicing Patience: Action Items

A study by Northwestern University found that people who used their nondominant hand for simple tasks for two weeks developed better control over their anger (Denson, DeWall, and Finkel, 2012). Why? It forced them to slow down and think about what they were doing. Consider adopting this strategy or some other means of slowing yourself down before you respond. Being patient and slowing down for as little as fifty to a hundred milliseconds before acting gives the brain time to process information and respond more intentionally and rationally (Teichart, Ferrera, and Grinband, 2014).

> Visualization techniques like the one Carl from the case study used can be tremendously helpful. When you feel angry, imagine the wave of anger cresting and falling. Wait until the wave has rolled onto shore before acting.

> Classic strategies such as fasting, regular confession, and offering a brief prayer before speaking in general and especially in difficult circumstances combine the benefits of the previous, more psychological techniques with the grace that God gives us to do more than we ever could do if we were working under our own power.

All of these activities can improve your ability to pause and think before you respond, an essential part of both problem-solving (i.e, healthy, justice-seeking behavior) and cultivating the kind of patience we've been discussing in this chapter. What other ideas do you have? Write them here.

The Divine Longing for Justice: A Promise

For those of you whose divine longing for justice is crying out, know that you do not have to fight your battles alone. God is on your side. In fact, through the cross of Jesus Christ, God has already claimed the victory in all of your battles. Trust him. For blessed are you who hunger and thirst for justice.

Chapter Seven

Satisfying the Divine Longing for Peace

Peace demands the most heroic labor and the
most difficult sacrifice. It demands greater
heroism than war. It demands greater
fidelity to the truth and a much more
perfect purity of conscience.
—*Thomas Merton*

Peace. Who doesn't want more peace in their life? Our lives
are filled with conflict. Our hearts are consumed by ongoing
battles with that inner voice that won't stop picking, picking,
picking.

And in the middle of all of this chaos, conflict, and noise,
Jesus comes to give us the peace that we all long for.

Come to me, all you who are weary and burdened, and I
will give you rest. Take my yoke upon you and learn from
me, for I am gentle and humble in heart, and you will find
rest for your souls. For my yoke is easy and my burden is
light (Mt 11:28-30).

Peace I leave with you; my peace I give you. I do not give
to you as the world gives. Do not let your hearts be troubled and do not be afraid (Jn 14:27).

I have told you these things, so that in me you may have peace. In this world you will have trouble. But take heart! I have overcome the world (Jn 16:33).

Most of us find these words of Christ incredibly comforting, if not just a little difficult to believe. Since this world is anything but peaceful, it can be hard to hope that we could ever experience anything resembling peace in our lives. But deep within our hearts is a call to peace, a call that becomes stronger the closer we draw to God.

The Root of Our Longing for Peace

Like the divine longing for justice, the divine longing for peace is rooted in the collective unconscious memory of the Original Unity of God and humankind. As I have noted throughout this book, Original Unity is the term coined by St. John Paul the Great in his theology of the body (2006). It refers to the state of harmony that existed before the Fall, when God, man, and woman were in union with one another and all the world functioned according to God's intended design.

After the Fall, when sin entered the world, the peace and harmony of Original Unity was all but destroyed. Nothing worked as it should. Chaos, disorder, and discord reigned. Still, in God's mercy, humankind continues to be haunted by a deep longing for peace, not just the peace that comes from the absence of conflict and injustice in our own lives, but also the "peace of the interior gaze," when God, man, and woman were one and could be known intimately and harmoniously by one another.

Peace: The Longing Defined

As much as we desire peace, we are often confused about what it actually is. Ask a hundred people to tell you what they mean when they pray "Lord, give me peace!" and most will tell you that they just want to be left alone, to stop having to put up with all the stress and drama of the world. But avoidance isn't true peace. Avoiding problems and struggles can, at best, result in quiet, which can be understood as merely the absence of conflict. And although quiet has its place, it is not the same thing as peace.

The *Catechism of the Catholic Church* puts it this way:

> Peace is not merely the absence of war, and it is not limited to maintaining a balance of powers between adversaries. Peace cannot be attained on earth without safeguarding the goods of persons, free communication among men, respect for the dignity of persons and peoples, and the assiduous practice of fraternity. Peace is "the tranquillity of order." Peace is the work of justice and the effect of charity (*CCC,* no. 2304).

True peace takes work, sometimes hard work. It requires us to say the things that need to be said, to work for justice, to make sure people are treated with dignity and respect, and to ensure both my needs and yours are met in a manner that respects our common good.

Peace Versus Justice: The Difference

While there is some degree of overlap between the divine longing for justice and the divine longing for peace, there is an important distinction. The divine longing for justice enables us to become aware of the disorder around us and desire to take some sort of action to correct it. The divine longing for peace empowers us to *sustain* our effort, to *evaluate* our progress, to *adjust* course as necessary, and to *develop* new strategies as needed. If we were to imagine going on a voyage to a distant land across the sea, the divine longing for justice is what gets our ship to leave the harbor in the first place, while the divine longing for peace keeps us on course toward our destination and prevents us from turning around and going back home when the going gets tough.

Divinization and the Divine Longing for Peace

Of course, the divine longing for peace doesn't just point to harmony in this world. It also reminds us that true harmony will not be achieved until we have fulfilled our destiny through divinization. Our ability to experience ultimate peace, the peace that this world cannot give (Jn 14:27), depends on our pursuit of authentic union with God. St. Augustine once asked, "What good is peace in the world if we are at war with ourselves?" (Thigpen, 2001).

As Augustine's question suggests, even if we were able to resolve all of the world's problems (including the tensions in our own lives), if we were not able to achieve the unity within ourselves that can come only from having achieved union with God, our divine longing for peace would remain unsatisfied. True peace—especially the peace that comes from our quest to become the gods we were created to be—requires commitment, a sustained effort, and that's where things often break down.

How Sloth Distorts the Divine Longing for Peace

> The most deadly poison of our times is indifference.
> —*St. Maximilian Kolbe*

Sloth is the deadly sin that frustrates our ability to satisfy our divine longing for peace. We tend to think of sloth as simple laziness. We imagine it as the sin of sitting in front of the TV too much, taking too long a break, or wasting time, but there's more to it than that.

Sloth is the sin of indifference, of choosing not to try to improve a relationship or a situation I know to be unhealthy or unjust, either because I think it would be too hard, or just because I don't feel like it. Sloth is Satan's counterfeit of peace. Where peace is the harmony that exists because a problem has been satisfactorily resolved and, ultimately, greater union with God has been achieved, sloth is the attempt to eliminate tension, conflict, or complications by simply sticking one's head in the sand. Sloth is the sin of "not sweating the small stuff" and deciding that almost everything is small stuff.

David is a nice guy. Everyone likes him for his agreeable, easygoing nature. Unfortunately, he drives his wife, Lilly, crazy because he never offers an opinion about anything. "Whatever you want, Hon" is David's motto. Lilly often jokes that she's going to have those words engraved on his tombstone.

"At first I thought he was just being generous and deferential," Lilly says. "But it's getting to where I just don't feel like he cares about anything. It doesn't matter what I ask him, from 'What color would you prefer in the bedroom?' to 'Which school do you think the kids should go to?' It's always 'I don't know' or 'What do you think?' God forbid I try to bring up something contentious like the budget or his mother; he's totally allergic to conflict. He just completely shuts down, like a deer in the headlights. Sometimes I feel like I've married a ghost. I could really use a little less 'nice' and a lot more passion and investment in our lives."

Katelin is a nurse for a hospice program. Because hospice is intended to provide end-of-life care, the rules state that hospice can accept patients only if their doctors believe they have six months or less to live. Katelin has noticed that the director has been allowing many people who have serious chronic illnesses into the program. Many of these people are struggling with serious problems, but they could live for many years and could be better served by programs other than hospice. Katelin is concerned that the director is padding their census and, potentially, committing insurance fraud. Despite this, she has decided to turn a blind eye and not even ask the director to explain why these patients are being admitted. "It's my job to provide patient care. I'm there to help people, not make waves," Katelin says.

David and Katelin are both settling for sloth in an attempt to satisfy their longing for true peace. Neither of them is doing what they could to engage in their lives and address the issues that are right in front of them. David thinks that the key to a peaceful life is refusing to rock the boat even a little. He has allowed himself to become a total nonperson in order to maintain the quiet life he mistakes for a peaceful one, and in the process he is alienating his wife. For her part, Katelin believes that there are serious problems in her workplace, and while she may not bear any responsibility for the decisions that are made by the hospice administrator, she is complicit with the structures of sin in her workplace by refusing to even ask for clarification about why certain patients are being admitted.

It would be easy to criticize David and Katelin, except that we've all been guilty of similar sins of omission. How often do we agree with others just to get along? How many times do we see a problem at home, or at work, or in our parish, or in our community but we refuse to do even the little we could because we just don't need the hassle? How often do we see a person close to us hurting, but we turn a blind eye because we're just too tired to deal with whatever is bothering them? And why do we do it? Is it because we're "bad people"? I think it's too easy to come to that conclusion, and anyway it's not at all true. We don't commit such sins of omission because we want to be bad; we commit them because we long for peace—"the tranquillity that comes from right order"—but we tell ourselves that such a peace is neither possible nor worth the effort, so we settle for quiet.

I want to be clear. Some situations do call for patience. As we saw in our discussion of the divine longing for justice, sometimes we do need to let our good efforts mature, and that requires us to step away, wait, and watch for a time. But that's different from refusing to do what we could to address a situation that is disturbing the peace.

Classically, sloth is known by the more technical name *acedia,* which is defined as running away from the opportunity to discern or do what would be good. Sloth separates us from God's call to divinization because it prevents us from asking what God might want us to do, out of either complete disregard for God's will or because we're afraid that if we asked him what he wanted he might actually tell us. It is one thing if through thoughtful prayer, careful discernment, and responsible consultation we consciously decide that it would be better to leave something alone. It is another thing to simply fail to consider the question in the first place out of a desire to avoid trouble.

The Heavenly Virtue of Diligence: The Antidote to Sloth

Diligence is the virtue that both defeats sloth and helps us actualize our divine longing for peace by activating our gifts to respond to the problems we face, and by helping us stay the course when, inevitably, things don't go as smoothly as we planned. As St. Charles Borromeo reminds us,

> If we wish to make any progress in the service of God we must begin every day of our life with new eagerness. We must keep ourselves in the presence of God as much as possible and have no other view or end in all our actions but the divine honor (Boston Catholic.org (n.d.).

When we are confronted by threats to our peace, rather than exercising diligence, we often experience the sense that "there's nothing I could possibly do about this."

Brenda was estranged from her adult daughter, Maddie, who was living with her boyfriend. Brenda felt a deep sense of shame about her daughter's betrayal of the values she had been taught and an even deeper sense of frustration that her daughter seemed to be pushing her away, especially when Brenda tried to give her any advice.

"I don't know what to do," Brenda said. "I just feel so powerless. I can't accept the way she's choosing to live, but nothing I say makes any difference to her. I feel like giving up."

Instead of giving up, Brenda came to me for counseling to deal with the sadness and anger she was feeling over the breakdown in her previously close relationship with her daughter. I suggested that she might reclaim a sense of power by backing off from her attempts to argue her daughter into submission and, instead, focus on rebuilding her relationship in whatever ways her daughter was willing to allow. She took my advice, and over the course of several months tried to spend time with her daughter in whatever ways her daughter was open to. They went to lunch. They saw a movie together. They talked on the phone. Although it practically killed her, Brenda refrained from bringing up Maddie's cohabitation. Instead, she prayed that the Holy Spirit would work through her witness and through the relationship she was cultivating. She gave the situation to God, and when she found that her feelings were causing her to take the situation back onto herself, she would hand it over to God again.

After several months of this, Brenda came back to me to share her joy that she and her daughter were in a much better place and that Maddie was coming around on her own about faith issues. Maddie started asking Brenda about church. Their conversations led Maddie to look into RCIA (the process by which a person comes into the Catholic Church as an adult) for both her and her boyfriend. Brenda was beside herself.

"There's still a long way to go, I know," Brenda said, "but I'm just so happy to see that she is open. I'm so glad God got us to this better place and was able to use my relationship with Maddie to do something good in her life."

When Brenda first came to me, she was ready to give up on her relationship with her daughter. She felt powerless. She felt that the only thing left to do was to cut her daughter off and isolate herself. Yet her willingness to be diligent in the face of this temptation enabled her to discover that being present with Maddie was a gift she could give to her daughter. By opening up her heart and continuing to persevere in prayer despite the frustration she experienced, Brenda was able to be a conduit of grace in Maddie's life. It ended up that as Maddie and her boyfriend went through RCIA they decided to live apart for a time, at the pastor's suggestion, while they discerned marriage. Eventually, they decided to get married in the church shortly after they were both received into the church.

Not every situation works out so perfectly. That's not the point. The true purpose of this story is to highlight that when we refuse to give in to the temptation to act as if we're powerless and instead remain diligent, we open up channels of grace through which God's spirit can work. When we do this, transformation occurs not just in our environment but in our hearts and in the hearts of those around us. Brenda's situation didn't involve open conflict, but even when we are involved in open conflicts we are called to be diligent instruments of grace.

Diligence and Staying the Course

Peter came to counseling because he wanted to fix his troubled marriage. At least part of the problem was that while his wife, Fiona, had very strong opinions about how things should be, Peter was content to check out of the relationship and let her make all the decisions. In time, Peter learned how to find his voice and start giving her the feedback Fiona said she wanted. But his efforts didn't pay off as he had expected.

"We had another huge fight," Peter said. "All these years I've had to hear about how I never have an opinion and how Fi wants a partner, but God forbid I actually say something. Then there's all kinds of hell to pay. She'll never be happy."

First I asked Peter whether the goal was making Fiona happy or becoming a healthier person and a better partner. I explained that if it was the former, then he might spend his life jumping through hoops, since people are often more fickle than we'd like them to be. On the other hand, if his goal was to learn to be a healthier person and a better partner, he needed to admit to himself that he was on the right track, and maybe this was the point in the relationship where he needed to help Fiona become the partner she said she wanted to be.

He acknowledged that there was something to what I was saying. "Fiona's parents argued constantly," he said. "I never saw them agree on any decision. Now that you mention it, I suspect Fi would like us to be partners, but she doesn't really have much more of an idea of how to create that than I do. Neither of us grew up in that kind of home."

With my encouragement, the next time Fiona got upset at Peter for expressing his opinion, Peter reminded her that she used to constantly complain about wanting a partner. "I told her, 'Look, I'm finally trying to be the person you always said you needed me to be, and you're killing it. I need us to work together to learn how to . . . well, work together.'"

Peter invited Fiona to join him in marriage counseling, and together they were able to learn how they could use each other's opinions to create new, mutually satisfying solutions to whatever challenge they faced.

Making changes isn't easy. Peter felt tremendously justified in being angry that Fiona wasn't following through on what she claimed to want for their marriage. Emotionally, it would have made sense for him to give up. But by making a commitment to remain diligent, both he and Fiona grew in the virtues that enabled them to have both a more meaningful and a more intimate marriage.

Diligence and Divinization

Proverbs 4:23 reminds us, "Watch over your heart with all diligence, for from it flow the springs of life." Any good goal worth pursuing requires persistence and diligence to achieve, so the goal of becoming partakers in God's divine nature requires even more of the same. When we look at life with eyes of faith, we see that diligently and faithfully responding to the mundane challenges of everyday life has eternal ramifications. In the words of Archbishop Fulton Sheen, "Every moment comes to you pregnant with divine purpose!" Conventional wisdom tells us not to sweat the small stuff, and while it is true that we must be careful not to turn common trials and challenges into catastrophes, that's different from acting as if nothing matters. In every moment of every day, God is working mightily to use every means at his disposal to transform us into the divine beings we were meant to be so that we might share eternity with him. Our divine longing for peace will be fully satisfied only when we are reunited with God, and the original harmony that existed between God and humanity is restored. We can at least begin working toward that union by diligently offering our gifts and talents to every situation we encounter. Every time we choose to reject sloth's temptation to *powerlessness* and instead diligently act in a manner that intentionally brings God's grace to bear on the situations we face, we take a step toward restoring the order in which God intended us to live. In doing so, we experience a tranquillity that satisfies our divine longing for peace.

Satisfying the Divine Longing
for Peace: An Exercise

PRAY

Lord Jesus Christ,

You are the source of the peace beyond all understanding. Help me to remember, Lord, that true peace can be achieved only by seeking right order. Give me the diligence I need both to use my gifts more fully and to persevere despite the obstacles and frustrations I encounter. Help me to remember that you have called me to be your presence in the world. Help me to engage more fully so that I might experience a more abundant life in this world and the next. I ask this through Jesus Christ my Lord. Amen.

COAL: Fuel for Change

As you consider ways in which you could more effectively satisfying your divine longing for peace, take a moment to consider how COAL can help fuel the changes you would like to make in your life.

CURIOSITY AND OPENNESS

Ask yourself: Where did I learn that the best way to get through life was to shut down or check out?

> Who taught me this response?

> What situations impressed this lesson on me?

> Do I want to continue to allow these experiences to rule my life?

Do not judge or edit yourself. Receive your answers in a spirit of openness and grace.

ACCEPTANCE

Say, "These are the experiences that have shaped my struggle to satisfy my divine longing for peace. I accept my past even as I accept God's call to change and grow."

LOVE

Loving myself means working to become the person God wants me to be. I know that I can fulfill my deepest longing for peace only by being diligent in the face of the disorder around me.

> What specific situations in my life would benefit from my being more diligent in working to restore right order?
>
> What obstacles would I have to overcome to achieve this goal?
>
> What help, resources, or support might I need to overcome these obstacles?
>
> Say, "I will love myself and accept God's love for me by choosing this path of diligence over the temptation to sloth."

Review these loving resolutions each morning. Imagine a time in the coming day when you might be tempted to sloth. Imagine responding instead with diligence. Ask for God's help to remember this more loving response in those times when you are feeling tempted to shut down or withdraw from the things happening right in front of you.

Practicing Diligence: Action Items

Increasing your capacity for diligence to satisfy your divine longing for peace requires two things. First, you need to increase your awareness of how your gifts (including your time, treasure, talent, and even your body) can be used to make the lives of others around you better. Second, you need to learn to keep up your efforts in the face of obstacles.

TO INCREASE AWARENESS

When you enter a room, ask yourself: What is one thing I can do to leave this room in better shape than I found it?

Each day, ask yourself: What will I do to make the life of one person I know a little easier today?

TO SUSTAIN YOUR EFFORTS

Each day, ask yourself: What is one problem the people around me are concerned with? What is one small thing I can do to generate a new idea for solving this problem or one small step I can take to effect a solution?

At the end of each day, write one or two sentences on what you did that day to try to address this problem by gathering new information, suggesting a new idea, or making some small effort to resolve it.

Write one or two sentences on the obstacles you encountered (from either inside or outside yourself) as you tried to address the problem.

Write one or two sentences about how you might overcome that obstacle (e.g., by gathering new information, talking to the person who got in your way, seeking more training or professional assistance, etc.).

Write one sentence describing the action step you will attempt tomorrow in order to take another step forward. Then look at your schedule or smart device and create an appointment to accomplish this task.

The Divine Longing for Peace: A Promise

As you have seen throughout this chapter, the divine longing for peace is not achieved by sitting down and taking a load off. It can be achieved only by first becoming prayerfully aware of the changes God wishes to make in and through you and then applying yourself diligently to making those changes so that you can live a more abundant life in both this world and the next. As St. Gerard Majella put it, "Who except God can give you peace? Has the world ever been able to satisfy the heart?"

You can hope to truly satisfy the divine longing for peace only if you can leave behind the temptation to try to arrange a life that is small enough that you can manage on your own (there is no such thing) and instead embrace the largesse of the life God wants for you. But in doing so, you will get more than you bargained for. Not only will you become a powerful agent of change and grace; you will draw closer and closer to fulfilling your ultimate destiny by conforming yourself more and more to the image of the same God who said, "Peace I leave with you; my peace I give to you" (Jn 14:27).

Chapter Eight

Satisfying the Divine Longing for Trust

[The Christian life requires] firm trust in the Holy Spirit, for it is he who "helps us in our weakness" (Rom 8:26). . . . It is true that this trust in the unseen can cause us to feel disoriented: it is like being plunged into the deep and not knowing what we will find. . . . Yet there is no greater freedom than that of allowing oneself to be guided by the Holy Spirit, renouncing the attempt to plan and control everything to the last detail, and instead letting him enlighten, guide and direct us, leading us wherever he wills. The Holy Spirit knows well what is needed in every time and place.

—*Pope Francis,* The Joy of the Gospel

What a joy it would be to be able to trust! How good would it feel to give up the fear that everything is up to us? To stop flogging ourselves to run faster and work harder so that we can stay ahead of the bill collectors, the unexpected storms of misfortune, the hostile forces that seem to be allied against us? To believe that God really does desire and is prepared to meet all of our needs (Phil 4:19)?

The Root of Our Longing

Like all of the divine longings, our divine longing for trust is rooted in humankind's pre-fallen experience in the Garden. We are told in Genesis 2:15 that man was created, in part, because the soil needed to be tilled. Christian tradition holds that work before the Fall was a dignified, profitable, and enjoyable affair. God was a good boss—so to speak—and because of the harmony that existed between God, the world, and humankind, Adam could trust that the earth would respond to his care, producing everything our first parents needed.

The *Catechism of the Catholic Church* speaks about God's original intention behind work, which is very different from how many of us experience work today.

> Human work proceeds directly from persons created in the image of God and called to prolong the work of creation by subduing the earth, both with and for one another . . . (*CCC,* no. 2427).

> In work, the person exercises and fulfills in part the potential inscribed in his nature. The primordial value of labor stems from man himself, its author and its beneficiary. Work is for man, not man for work (*CCC,* no. 2428).

The kind of work our first parents did in the Garden and of which the *Catechism* speaks is the kind of work that enables us to feel accomplished because we're engaging in meaningful pursuits that challenge and stretch us in the best ways and help us to become everything we are created to be. This kind of work is infused with the trust that our work befits our dignity, that our needs will be provided for, that our efforts will pay off, and that we have nothing to fear because our work is blessed by the God who will meet all of our needs.

Jesus affirms this call to trust when he reminds us,

> "Therefore I tell you, do not worry about your life and what you will eat, or about your body and what you will wear. . . . Notice the ravens: they do not sow or reap; they have neither storehouse nor barn, yet God feeds them. How much more important are you than birds! Can any of you by worrying add a moment to your life-span? If even the smallest things are beyond your control, why are you anxious about the rest? Notice how the flowers grow. They do not toil or spin. But I tell you, not even Solomon in all his splendor was dressed like one of them. If God so clothes the grass in the field that grows today and is thrown into the oven tomorrow, will he not much more provide for you, O you of little faith?" (Lk 12:22-28).

Note Jesus's use of the word "toil" (Lk 12:27). Toil is a very different kind of work. We first encounter that word *after* the Fall, in Genesis 3:17-19:

> Because you listened to your wife and ate from the tree
>   about which I commanded you, you shall not eat
>   from it
> Cursed is the ground because of you!
> In toil you shall eat its yield
> all the days of your life.
> Thorns and thistles it shall bear for you,
> and you shall eat the grass of the field.
> By the sweat of your brow
> you shall eat bread.

After the Fall, when the delicate balance between God, the world, and humankind was disrupted, work got a new name, "toil." Sin entered the world and the harmony that characterized our labors no longer existed. Our efforts no longer produce the fruit they once did. *Toil is, essentially, work stripped of our trust* that the things we are asked to do are not beneath us, that our needs will be provided for, and that our efforts will, in fact, pay off.

And yet, though this natural ability to easily trust in God's Providence has been largely lost to us, a part of our collective unconscious remembers and aches for a return to our original state, a state in which we had confidence that we could know that the work God was asking us to do was consistent with our dignity, and that through our good efforts God would supply all that we need. This ache represents the divine longing for trust.

Greed: The Distortion of the Divine Longing for Trust

> Then he said to the crowd, "Take care to guard against all greed, for though one may be rich, one's life does not consist of possessions" (Lk 12:15).

Although we ache to trust God, we often fail. We are too afraid to trust, so we grasp at whatever we can reach that will calm our fears. Rather than running into the perfect love of God that will cast out every fear, we run, pell-mell, toward whatever we can grasp at—money, valuables, status. Toddlers have security blankets and adults buy securities. Both give a similar illusion of safety, but they are only illusions. Fear is an unavoidable consequence of the Fall. Like our post-fallen, first parents, we are naked and we know it. God longs to quell our fears. All we have to do is let him draw us closer into the safety of his arms. He asks us to trust him, but we settle for greed.

Greed is our response to the fear that, despite the sum of his promises to the contrary, God is getting ready to drop us at any moment. Greed distorts the divine longing for trust because by putting so many things in our own hands, we can no longer hold God's. Greed shouts that it is entirely up to us to take care of ourselves however we can, and if that means sacrificing our dignity, our health, our relationships, and our humanity, then so be it.

Greed tells us that we can never have enough. The mother of a good friend of mine grew up during the Great Depression. She often told my friend vivid stories about walking home from school and passing yet another set of neighbors who had been evicted, sitting on the sidewalk surrounded by the few possessions they had left. Although she made it through the Depression relatively unscathed because of her father's position as the superintendent of an apartment building, my friend's mother lived her life traumatized by the memory of her friends sitting on the sidewalk in despair. As an adult, my friend's mother became a workaholic who was never home. My friend essentially raised himself because both his mother and father were too busy staying ahead of the sword that they feared was constantly hanging over their heads despite their comfortable life. As my friend puts it, "I try to be grateful that I never wanted for any material needs, but my gratitude often gets crowded out by how much I wanted to feel that they loved me."

The fact is, this fear is not entirely irrational. Fortunes, no matter what size they are, can be easily wiped out. People do suffer. There is want in the world. But greed tells us that we can insulate ourselves from it all. We don't need to trust God; we just have to work harder, and harder, and harder still; and if we can work hard enough, and hoard what we earn from our labors (no matter how little or how much that may be), we can outrun the reaper *all on our own*.

So does this mean that saving money or being financially blessed is, in itself, bad? Of course not. The context of the parable of the Rich Fool makes that clear (Lk 12:13-21). The rich man wasn't foolish because he was happy that his crops did well that year or because he wanted to save what he harvested, or even because he wanted to enjoy the fruits of his labor. He was foolish because he believed that his good fortune meant that he was so self-sufficient that he no longer had to depend upon God or be considerate to his fellow man. That's why the parable ends, in verse 21, with Jesus saying, *"Thus will it be for the one who stores up treasure for himself but is not rich in what matters to God."* We won't be condemned for having things; what will condemn us is our belief that those things can be our salvation.

There is very little in our life that is within our ability to control, and trying to deny this by working ourselves to death, shutting people out, and keeping everything to ourselves is foolish at best and terminally destructive to body and soul at worst.

Greed and the Illusion of Control

A hospital chaplain I know works with people who have experienced critical trauma in their lives. Whether they are reeling from a loss related to a car accident, plane crash, cat-astrophic storm, or a terminal diagnosis, one of the things he says people struggle with the most is the loss of their sense of control.

"I have found it helpful to ask the people I care for to tell me about a time in their lives when they really were in con-trol," he says. "They usually start by relating some situation or another when things were going well. I listen, but when they're done, I ask them, 'But were you really in control?' Inevitably, they come to realize what I'm getting at. Good things come. Bad things come. We aren't really in control of any of it at any moment, especially when we think we are. We can try to do what we can to put the odds in our favor, but that isn't the same thing as being in control, and those efforts can be just as easily swept away in a heartbeat. The only thing we can place our trust in is the constancy of God. If we forget his presence and Providence, everything else is an illusion."

It is terrifying for most of us to be forced to confront the reality of our utter lack of control over anything at any time, but I think it can also be profoundly liberating if we allow it to be. When we can accept that we control nothing, we are free to stop spending our lives in useless pursuits. If we can control nothing, then why not stop running around and listen to God, who is in control of everything? If we control noth-ing, what do we have to lose if we stop trying to follow our own will and, instead, ask God what his will for us might be? If working obsessively hard isn't a guarantee that we can stave off misfortune, why not work in more humane ways that re-spect our dignity and protect our relationships? If we can't guarantee our ability to really hold on to anything we have no matter how we try to hoard it, why not share what we have with those who are in need?

The Heavenly Virtue of Generosity:
The Antidote to Greed

> Charity is the form, mover, mother and root of all the virtues.
>
> —*St. Thomas Aquinas*

Generosity (or charity) is the authentic means of addressing the ache that is our divine longing for trust. Many people think of generosity or charity as something we do for other people. Most of us—myself included—are fairly self-centered. We don't particularly like doing anything if we can't see that it has a direct benefit for us. Despite the fact that, superficially, charity is about other people, generosity is really an act of brave defiance. When we are generous to others with our treasure, talent, and time, we laugh in the face of Satan, who wants to persuade us that giving of ourselves will result in our doom. The reason St. Thomas Aquinas calls charity the "form, mover, mother and root of all the virtues" is that being charitable reminds us that God gives us everything we have so that we can use it to work for the good of others. When we practice defiant acts of charity and generosity, we stare at the gun Satan points at our heads, the gun loaded with bullets of want, lack, fear, and chaos, and instead of cowering, we laugh at him and begin to dance.

There are few things braver than charity. If you doubt it, think of the feeling you get when the collection basket comes around. Assuming that doing so wouldn't actually prevent you from paying your bills, what could be braver than defying that natural tendency to root around in your wallet for the smallest bill and instead donating what you are actually capable of giving? Do you think, for one minute, that it isn't Satan we're fighting with as we scrounge around for the smallest amount we can give? If battling the devil doesn't demand bravery, I don't know what does.

What you actually give to the church or any other charity is between you and God. That said, however much you give, the reason we tend not to give as much as we could is because of greed, the fear that if we don't hold on to everything we can, we might not be okay.

Generosity is the virtue that challenges us to overcome this grasping fear. Moreover, despite the fact that others benefit from our acts of charity, we are the greatest beneficiaries. A major study by the University of British Columbia found that when given the choice to spend money on themselves or others, people who are more financially generous to others are significantly happier than people who spend the same amount on themselves (Dunn, Aknin, and Norton, 2014). This study builds on a wider body of literature that finds that giving to others greatly enhances the benefactor's sense of well-being and happiness. In fact, the authors of the UBC study, in their summary of prior research, noted that generosity may be a key to universal well-being. In particular, they noted research that shows how generosity benefits brain function by stimulating the reward centers of the brain and decreasing the production of the stress chemical, cortisol (Harbaugh, Mayr, and Burghart, 2007; Dunn, Ashton-James, Hanson, and Aknin, 2010), and has been demonstrated to increase the happiness of people all over the world, regardless of whether they are rich or poor. It is as close to an established fact as you can get in the social sciences: the more you give what you can to benefit others, the happier you are. In fact, although researchers found that people who give money are happier than people who don't give anything, people who give both money and time are even happier than those who give money alone!

This leads to a second way we can be generous to others: by being present. Earlier in the book, I shared the story of my friend who took the time to not only give a homeless man a few dollars but also made the effort to learn his name and find out how the man took his coffee. My friend's willingness to be present in that moment and refuse to treat the man as merely a charity case but as a person, set him apart from many others. We may give from our resources, but our presence and our willingness to make the time for relationship is the gift that matters more.

Being generous with our money and time helps to satisfy our divine longing for trust because we are demonstrating that we accept the lack of control we have in life, and we are connecting with the perfect love of God that casts out the fear that makes us hold on to everything we have "just in case." We are embracing God's call to be as generous to others as he is to us. If others can count on us to be generous to them, with all our weakness, fears, and imperfections, how much more can we count on God to be generous with his abundant treasure in this life and the next?

Generosity and Divinization

As we become more generous to others and, in turn, reflect on God's generosity to us, we eventually must turn our attention to the incredible generosity that God displays in his desire to share with us his most precious gift: his divinity. He wants to make us gods! By what right can we claim such a gift? How could we earn it? Of course, it's impossible to lay claim to deification on our own, but God in his infinite generosity longs to make it so.

Reflecting on this ultimate act of generosity begins to satisfy our divine longing for trust in two more ways that affect us on an even deeper level. First, reflecting on God's desire to share his divinity with us drives home the realization that if God would share such an unbelievable gift with us, what would he deny us? I don't mean to imply that if you pray for a mansion and a yacht God will give them to you. But what I do mean is that if God is willing to share the gift of his divinity with us, would he fail to help us find a way to pay our electric bill? In light of the gift of divinization, it's absurd that we fret so much over so many things. That's not to say that we should sit around and wait for things to fall into our laps. As Scripture says, those who are *unwilling* to work also should not eat (2 Thes 3:10). *Of course* we have to work to meet our expenses, but maybe, in light of the gift of God's divinity, we could allow ourselves to work in a manner that is more in line with our dignity and our relationships. Maybe we could trust what Scripture tells us: "Work at your tasks in due season, and in his own time God will give you your reward" (Sir 51:30).

Second, reflecting on the gift of God's divinity reminds us of the deep level at which he wants to satisfy our divine longing for trust. It is as if, knowing that we have a hard time trusting him, God says, "Look, you're always bugging me about these little things you need, and no matter how much I say, 'I got this,' you doubt me. How about I do something so crazy, so impossible, so unbelievable, that if you grasp it, you'll never doubt me again? Would you like that?" And then he takes our hand and starts transforming us into gods.

Divinization requires radical trust. As we established in the earlier chapters of this book, to think that we—in our brokenness, sinfulness, and imperfections—could aspire to become gods is laughable, if not outright offensive. Except that's exactly what God has told us he intends to do. Although in reality we control nothing and can guarantee less, we can at least uphold the illusion that we have the power to pay our water bills on our own. Be that as it may, there is no illusion outside of delusion that says we could turn ourselves into gods. But the more generous we are to others, the more we are able to get in touch with the radical generosity of God and believe, even though it is truly impossible to comprehend, that God intends to make us like him, both perfect and eternal. If we who are imperfect can use every part of ourselves to work for the good of others, how much more can our Father in heaven use every part of himself to work wonders in our lives (see Lk 11:13)?

This is exactly why those who progress along the *illuminative way* and the *unitive way* in their spiritual walk experience less and less anxiety and greater and greater trust. The farther we travel down that spiritual path that leads to divinization, the more real the idea of God's promise to make us partakers in his divinity looks to us. The more apparent this becomes, the more ridiculous it seems to worry about every other concern or desire, which pales by comparison. We can find the fullest satisfaction of our divine longing for trust only by drawing closer to God and realizing that there is no part of himself that he holds back from us. He is ours and we are his. By accepting his generosity in our own hearts and then letting this generosity inspire us to be as fully generous to others as our circumstances permit, we begin walking the path that satisfies one of the deepest longings of the human heart: the desire to trust, to, as the saying goes, "let go and let God."

Satisfying Your Divine Longing
for Trust: An Exercise

PRAY

Lord Jesus Christ,

Through your passion, death, and resurrection, you give me everything and make it possible for me to become a partaker in your divine nature. I accept your gift. Come into my heart more and more each day and as you do, inspire me to give myself fully to the people in my life. Let me look for ways to give more of my time, presence, and treasure to those I live with, and those I meet throughout my day. Give me a heart that burns with generosity so that I may surrender the illusion of control in my life and trust nothing more than I trust in you. You are my all in all, and I trust my life, my work, my relationships, my well-being, and my eternity to your loving care. I ask this through Jesus Christ my Lord. Amen.

COAL: Fuel for Change

As you reflect on ways you can satisfy your divine longing for trust, take a moment to consider how COAL can help fuel the changes you would like to make in your life.

CURIOSITY AND OPENNESS

Ask yourself: Where did I learn that I need to "take care of myself" and that the best way to do this is by working to an excessive degree or hoarding what I earn?

> Who taught me this response?
>
> What situations impressed this lesson on me?
>
> Do I want to continue to allow these experiences to rule my life?

Do not judge or edit yourself. Receive your answers in a spirit of openness and grace.

ACCEPTANCE

Say, "These are the experiences that have shaped my struggle to satisfy my divine longing for trust. I accept my past even as I accept God's call to change and grow."

LOVE

Loving myself means working to become the person God wants me to be. I know that I can fulfill my deepest longing for trust only by being generous and charitable in the face of the struggles I encounter.

> In what specific areas of my life do I feel my conscience—the voice of God in my heart—calling me to be more generous with my time, presence, or treasure?
>
> What obstacles would I have to overcome to achieve this goal?
>
> What help, resources, or support might I need to overcome these obstacles?

Say, "I will love myself and accept God's love for me by choosing this path of generosity over the temptation to greed."

Review these loving resolutions each morning. Imagine a time in the coming day when you might be tempted to greed. Imagine responding instead with generosity. Ask for God's help to remember this more loving response in those times when you are being tempted to refuse to share your time or your treasure with others.

Practicing Generosity: Action Items

Develop a devotion to the Divine Mercy of God. St. Faustina's constant prayer was "Jesus, I trust in you." Praying the Chaplet of Divine Mercy can help us to trust in God's generous plan for us and inspire us to be similarly generous to others. You can learn more about devotion to Jesus's Divine Mercy at www.thedivine mercy.org.

> Blessed Teresa of Calcutta once told a wealthy woman who wanted to be more charitable that when she went shopping for a new sari, she should choose two she liked, buy the less expensive one, and give the difference to the poor. What are some ways you could practice this idea in your life the next time you go shopping for clothes, housewares, or even a car or a home?

Prayerfully reflect on your finances. Consult with a financial planner about how much you could reasonably give to charitable pursuits after you consider your needs and the needs of those who depend upon you (including a rightly ordered need to enjoy the life God has given you). Slowly and prayerfully, work toward increasing how much you allocate to charitable pursuits each month.

Prayerfully reflect on how you spend your time. How might you be a little more generous with the time you spend with the people in your life? Go through the following list and write down approximately how much time you spent with the following people over the course of a week:

—Your spouse:

—Your children:

—Your co-workers:

—Other people you meet throughout the day:

Review your responses each day and ask yourself how mindful you were about opportunities to be more present to the people who share your life. Once you have mastered these initial goals, consider additional ways you might be more generous with your time and presence to the people you encounter throughout your day.

The Divine Longing for Trust: A Promise

Through all the chaos and storms of life, the divine longing for trust reminds us that the impossible is possible. We can stop worrying. We can stop working ourselves to death. We can stop hoarding. We can afford to be generous with our time and presence and the material things God has given us. And, finally, we can trust that God has amazing plans for our lives and that, specifically, he intends to take the most broken, hurting, despicable parts of ourselves and transform them so that we will be able to give ourselves as freely and totally to God as he gives himself to us.

Throw yourself into the loving arms of God, who wants nothing more than to provide for every physical, emotional, relational, and spiritual need; who longs to fill all the gaps in your life, including, most of all, the space that exists between his heart and yours. Every moment of every day, let each breath cry out with the words of St. Faustina: "Jesus, I trust in you!" And feel the loving, generous presence of God filling your life and transforming you into the generous image of his very own face.

Chapter Nine

Satisfying the Divine Longing for Well-Being

In uniting yourself to God's will, you take on new
life and gather great courage, willingly embracing
the cross and kissing His hand . . . , a hand that
reaches out to you in love and has no other
intention but your greater spiritual well-being.
—*St. Paul of the Cross*

"Be well."

A friend expressed this wish to me the other day as I was
leaving his home. It was an honest, albeit casual, good-bye
that conveyed his desire that all would be right with me until
our paths crossed once again.

Being well is something we all wish for. No one longs to
be ill, to be "out of order," so to speak. We all want to lead
lives that are healthy, happy, whole, and filled with meaningful connection to others. And we will go to great lengths to
achieve well-being. We all want to thrive.

Well-Being Defined

"Thriving" is another word for "well-being." When we say, "I
don't want to just survive, I want to thrive," we usually mean,
"I don't want to limp along as a disjointed collection of unmet

and conflicted needs. I want to experience peace, wholeness, and fulfillment in every area of my life."

Psychologists define thriving as the harmonious interplay of five different dimensions of well-being (Feeney and Collins, 2014):

1. *Hedonic well-being* has to do with the enjoyment you get from your life. It is different from the pleasure-driven (hedonic) happiness we discussed in our examination of abundance in chapter 4. Hedonism tends to be destructive, but hedonic well-being results from the pursuit of *healthy* pleasures. If you know how to enjoy yourself in healthy ways, have a good sense of humor and compelling hobbies, and try to consciously and intentionally take pleasure in the simple joys of daily life, you can be said to have a healthy degree of hedonic well-being.

2. *Eudaimonic well-being* is the joy of living a purposeful life (Boniwell, 2012). If you have a meaningful spiritual life and value system, if you feel that you are using your gifts to work for the good of others, can identify the small ways you are making a difference in the world, and enjoy the warmth of knowing that the people around you are genuinely better off because you are in their life, you are probably experiencing a strong sense of eudaimonic well-being.

3. *Psychological well-being* has to do with having a healthy, positive view of oneself combined with the absence of any mental health symptoms or disorders. If you like who you are as a person, feel good about your ability to set and meet positive goals for yourself, and are largely free of psychological/emotional problems that affect your abil-

ity to function well in your work, roles, and relationships, you probably exhibit a high degree of psychological well-being.

4. *Social well-being* involves having meaningful connections to people you care about and who care about you. If you feel that you can have faith in other people, that others are basically trustworthy; if you are affirmed by a group that shares your values and beliefs; and if you feel generally cared for by the people in your life, you probably have a high degree of social well-being.

5. *Physical well-being* encompasses physical strength and health. If you are fit and free of disease, are able to maintain appropriate activity levels, and are physically capable of doing all the activities that are important to you, you probably exhibit a high degree of physical well-being.

Very few people have achieved well-being across all five areas associated with *thriving*, but the degree to which you enjoy well-being in each of these five categories and hold them in balance is the degree to which you can say that you are thriving.

The Root of Our Longing

Because the desire for wellness is so universal and so deeply felt, it might not occur to us to think about where this divine longing for well-being comes from. After all, the state of the post-fallen person is anything but "well." Suffering, whether because of disease, stress, or conflict, is a much more familiar state of being for most of us than wellness, yet we don't dismiss the desire for well-being as a fantasy.

Perhaps it is because, as with all the other divine longings, a part of us remembers the wholeness humankind experienced before the Fall. In the chapter on the divine longing for peace, I shared St. Augustine's assertion that peace is the "tranquillity that results from right order." Before the Fall, all the world was at peace with itself and God because the world displayed the right order God intended when he created it. But there can be no peace in the world if there is no peace within our own hearts. Who among us has been able to maintain a peaceful spirit toward others when we have a toothache or are suffering from stress? Outer peace is the fruit of inner peace.

We can think of well-being, then, as the inner peace that results when the five dimensions of the self we defined above work together in balance. As Pope Paul VI wrote in *Populorum Progressio* (1967), "authentic human development concerns the whole of the person in every single dimension." We can say that we have achieved well-being to the degree that the whole of our person is well developed and held in balance (Siegel, 2012; Pargament, 2011).

After the Fall, we lost the ability to maintain that perfect balance between all the aspects of our physical, psychological, spiritual, and social self. In fact, I suspect many would say that most of the time these parts of ourselves are at war with one another. We want to pray, but we fall asleep. We want to take care of ourselves, but the people in our lives need to be cared for as well. We want to exercise, but we don't feel like it. We would like to fill our lives with the company of others, but their petty dramas wear us out. Each of us is a muddle of intentions working at cross-purposes.

It was not always so. In the beginning, there was unity between God and man and within man himself. Our first parents experienced this well-being, this perfectly balanced life, which resulted from inner and outer harmony. Across the millennia, this dimension of Original Unity calls out to us in the form of our divine longing for well-being, that deep ache we all experience for wholeness and health.

Gluttony: The Distortion of the Divine Longing for Well-Being

The world has redefined gluttony as the putative "sin" of being overweight. Gluttony is the new promiscuity. In a culture that celebrates lust as the ultimate virtue, the sin of "not being attractive enough" is the only vice worthy of condemnation.

For different reasons entirely, however, Christians have always recognized gluttony as a serious problem. Christians hold the body in high esteem. After all, we believe in the resurrection of the body. In his theology of the body, St. John Paul the Great recognizes that the body has not just biological significance but *theological* significance as well. He writes: "The body, and it alone, is capable of making visible what is invisible: the spiritual and the divine. It was created to transfer into the visible reality of the world the mystery hidden since time immemorial in God, and thus be a sign of it" (2006).

As a sign of respect for God's creation and because of its spiritual significance, Christianity clearly takes stewardship of the body very seriously, which is why gluttony has always been one of the capital sins. Gluttony undermines the healthy functioning and well-being not only of the body, but of the whole person as well. *It prevents us from living mindfully by substituting self-indulgence for self-care and by thwarting our call to be truly loving and accepting of our bodies as the gifts they are.*

Gluttony and Mindlessness

It would be easy to think of gluttony as indulgence in the "sin" of enjoying food. That doesn't really ring true to anyone who is the least bit familiar with Catholic culture. As the poem by historian and writer Hillaire Belloc cheekily asserts,

> Wherever the Catholic sun doth shine
> there is laughter and music and good red wine.
> At least I've always found it so.
> Benedicamus Domino!

Most spiritual authorities on the topic of gluttony object not so much to the pleasure we get from eating, or even from carrying a few extra pounds; instead they find fault with our tendency to eat mindlessly. In the words of St. Maximos the Confessor, "It is not food that is evil but gluttony, . . . it is only the misuse of things that is evil, and such misuse occurs when the intellect fails to cultivate its natural powers."

Likewise, in the words of St. Alphonsus Liguori,

> It is not a fault to feel pleasure in eating: for it is, generally speaking, impossible to eat without experiencing the delight which food naturally produces. But it is a defect to eat, like beasts, through the sole motive of sensual gratification, and without any reasonable object. Hence, the

most delicious meats may be eaten without sin, if the motive be good and worthy of a rational creature.

Remember that sin is accepting less than what God wants to give us (i.e., a "privation of the good"). Each of these saints notes that food and even the enjoyment of food can be a good thing. But too many of us eat for the same reason George Mallory climbed Mt. Everest: "Because it's there!" Unfortunately, the results are less admirable.

Eating in an unthinking manner, as the simplest animals do, essentially denies our humanity. If our destiny is to transcend our humanity and become gods through God's grace, we settle for a whole lot less when we deny not just our divine inheritance, but our basic humanity by approaching our food the way an animal does, eating it simply because we have an urge to.

But even this doesn't get at the deeper issue. As human beings, we are able to understand that our hunger is often about much more than a need for food. Nutritional experts know that the biggest cause of an unhealthy relationship with food is *emotional eating*, the attempt to satisfy an emotional, psychological, relational, or spiritual hunger with food or drink (Geliebter and Aversa, 2003).

When our relationships with the people in our lives, or our choices, or the ways we work, or think, or even pray (or don't) are unhealthy, we experience a dissatisfaction that makes us hunger for the well-being that we are lacking. But if we don't pause and consider what is driving us, it's easy to mistake this deeper hunger for a simple desire for food or drink. Continuing the addict's motto that we can't ever get enough of what we don't really want, we hope that the next trip to the fridge or the bar will fill the ache in the center of our being. We interpret that ache as hunger, and it is. But it is not a hunger for food or alcohol. It is a hunger to satisfy the divine longing for well-being, the desire to live a life in balance for the greater glory of God—a life that is considerate of our physical, emotional, relational, and spiritual well-being. St. Irenaeus once said that "the glory of God is man, fully alive"! When we live in a manner that pursues authentic well-being, our lives become works of art—living sculptures that glorify the sculptor by showing how, when we submit to the chisel of grace, every aspect of our lives can display the miraculous harmony in which God intended for us to live from the beginning of time.

Two Kinds of Gluttony: Overindulgence and Preciousness

Gluttony distorts our quest for well-being in two ironically contradictory ways: first, through *overindulgence,* that is, not caring enough about what we put into our bodies; second, by *preciousness,* that is, caring too much about how and what we eat. Both overindulgence and preciousness represent the problematic belief that salvation can come from our bodies and our senses. Let's take a brief look at both of them.

Gluttony Part I: Overindulgence

Anna's doctor is seriously concerned about her weight. She has stage 2 hypertension as well as several other weight-related health problems. She tried dozens of diets and even underwent Lap-Band surgery, but nothing worked. She admits that when she is dieting or even trying to curtail her eating a little she gets panicked feelings she doesn't understand. In speaking with her pastor, she came to realize that her unhappiness in her marriage was a huge trigger for her overeating. She would be fine all day, but when her husband came home she spent the rest of the evening stress-eating. She also explained that since she had put on so much weight, their sex life had dropped off to nothing. She told her pastor that she supposed she ought to feel bad about that, but it was a relief because she never really enjoyed sex with him anyway. Her pastor told her that through her weight problem God was challenging her to address her marital problems, and that she should seek counseling to heal her relationship. She thanked him for his encouragement but has yet to follow through. "I just don't see what good it would do," she said. "My husband and I have been like this for years. It's not like he's going to change, and I honestly don't think I have the energy to work on it anymore. Besides, marriage counseling is so expensive. I just don't know what the point would be." Meanwhile, her weight continues to skyrocket along with the health problems accompanying it.

Kirk lost his job six months ago. Since then he has stopped going to church. In fact, he has stopped doing a lot of things. He feels ashamed to be unemployed. He hates that his wife, a nurse anesthetist, is back at work. She keeps telling him that she's happy to do her part, but that just makes him even more miserable. He loves his kids, but the Mr. Mom role feels emasculating to him. Instead of trying to keep up with the house or sending out résumés, he surfs the Internet and plays video games while the kids are at school. When his wife asks him about his job search he gets angry and defensive. Most evenings, once his wife is home and is getting the kids to bed, he hangs out in the family room watching TV and drinking beer until he falls asleep. He denies he has a drinking problem. He just drinks to relax. It's the only time in his day he feels halfway decent. That doesn't feel like a problem to him.

Anna's hunger is really a hunger for intimacy and wholeness, but she's terrified to pursue what she really wants, either for fear that it won't work, or perhaps out of fear that it will, in which case she might have to make peace with her sexuality. Kirk is obviously depressed and consumed by crushing anxiety over his inability to be the provider he would like to be. That's completely understandable, but rather than reaching out to God in this difficult time, giving thanks for his wife's support, or seeking help to deal with his emotional struggles, he is retreating into alcohol abuse, wrapping the alcoholic buzz around himself like a security blanket that will chase all the monsters away. At least until the next morning.

How tempting is it for all of us to turn to food or drink when something in our lives is out of order? Gluttony as overindulgence makes us grasp for the refrigerator door or the wine glass when we are out of balance, instead of reaching out for God's hand waiting to right us on the path to our destiny. But there is a second, and ironically opposite, way that gluttony distorts our divine longing for well-being.

Gluttony Part II: Preciousness

There is a wonderful cartoon that shows Jesus, after multiplying the loaves and fishes, trying to feed the assembled throng. Instead of being grateful, the people depicted in the cartoon are saying things like "But I'm a vegan!" "Is that bread gluten-free?" "Has that fish been tested for mercury?"

Eating well is a good thing. No one disputes that good nutrition is important to our well-being. We *must* be intentional about what we put into our bodies. In fact, just as many disorders can be caused by poor eating habits, many health problems can be greatly improved or even eliminated altogether by eating properly. People with health problems are to be lauded if they seek the counsel of their physician or certified dietician to figure out how they can eat in a manner that can aid in their recovery.

But those people are a relatively small bunch. A much larger group of people, after reading an article or consulting Dr. Google one lazy evening in front of the computer, decide that all the problems in their life can be attributed to eating X. Or sometimes, X, Y, Z, P, D, and Q. If they could only eradicate all of these items from their diet, they would be saved. St. Thomas Aquinas referred to the tendency to be too particular about what one eats as *studiose,* or, in English, "preciousness," and he considered it a type of gluttony.

Individuals who are too careful about what they eat mean well, and their intentions are very, very good. But without realizing it, they fall into the same error as those who are overindulgent. Rather than looking into the imbalance in their life that might be causing the problems from which they seek relief, they want a back door that will relieve their pain. Looking for that secret health hack, they fall prey to the same belief that those guilty of overindulgence have: that salvation can come through the body.

And so, rather than just being intentional about what they eat, they make eating carefully a quasi-religion. Such well-meaning individuals may spend hours contemplating in the temples we know as health food and supplement stores. They religiously engage in sacred reading, carefully studying health books and periodicals. They seek out experts and gurus with questionable credentials who preach a gospel of long life, health, and happiness through deprivation. The popular cat-echist Fr. Robert Barron, remarking on this phenomenon, noted that, in his opinion, all the Puritans, with their belief in radical self-denial, grew up to become editors of health food and exercise magazines (Barron, 2007).

The problem, ironically, is that all this deprivation is so self-indulgent. Not only can it lead us into mindlessly ignor-ing other very real problems that require attention in our lives; it can also put up serious obstacles to relationship as people refuse to go to other people's homes because of what they might be tempted to eat or, alternatively, if they go out to a restaurant, they torment the poor waitress and kitchen staff and draw undue attention to themselves with a laundry list of special needs. Sometimes this cult of body worship can be offensive to relationship in more serious ways, as when health and fitness guru Jillian Michaels said that she would never get pregnant because, as she put it, "I can't handle doing that to my body" (*Huffington Post,* 2010). Our fascination with external appearance has made us a nation of people who are so dedicated to the cult of the body that they have forgotten that God intends the human body to be a visible sign of the love we were created to be and to give.

According to the National Eating Disorders Association, clinicians who treat eating disorders have coined the term *orthorexia* to describe the obsessive and disordered relationship to "eating right" (Kratina, n.d.). Eating disorder specialists note that orthorexia is on the rise and can be the cause of significant personal, emotional, and relational distress.

Francis came to counseling with a host of professional and personal issues. An attorney in group practice, he was "encouraged" to seek help by his partners. Colleagues said that Francis was insufferable in the break room because of his constant lecturing of staff about the various ways their lunches were poisoning their bodies. He would even criticize clients' eating habits, which led to several complaints to the senior partners in his firm.

Francis's marriage was also a shambles. He was so particular about his meals that his wife gave up trying to cook for him, and he rarely ate with the family, preferring to eat his own meals that he specially prepared for himself, or get takeout from a local restaurant that had items he would eat. Because of this, he often got home after the children were in bed. Because he was also training for a marathon, he spent a great deal of time on the weekends doing practice runs. All of this prevented him from having much of a relationship with his children at all. His wife often complained about being a single mother, and his children were suffering because of his absence.

Francis admitted to a counselor that he was very anxious, "high-strung" as he put it, and that he tended to react very strongly to even the smallest frustrations. He said that the other day, when his secretary was busy, he had to get a client file himself. That small incident snowballed, and he spent the day cataloging in his head all the different ways people tended to disappoint him. He often had difficulties getting to sleep because of such thoughts.

When the counselor asked about his relationship to food and exercise, Francis admitted that he had started eating the way he did to address his anxiety, and he felt that exercise was good for working out stress. In fact, the only time he didn't feel anxious was when he was exercising.

Asked by the counselor about goals, Francis surprised the therapist by ignoring all the emotional, relational, and professional complaints and asking, instead, for help to overcome his "addiction to diet soda." Francis said this was the one thing about his diet that he couldn't get a handle on and that he felt guilty about it. He felt sure that if he could stop putting those chemicals into his body, he might not be so anxious and stop feeling like a failure—at least when it came to his health and fitness, of which he was otherwise quite proud.

Francis is driven by good intentions. Tormented by the anxiety that rules his life, Francis is simply trying to find relief, but while diet and exercise can play an important part in finding relief from anxiety, he has simply transferred his anxious style of thinking and behaving to something he has total control over: the way he eats and exercises. Instead of dealing with the multiplicity of concerns and troubles in his professional, relational, and emotional life that are undermining his well-being, he is looking for salvation though his body and, in doing so, creating even more problems for himself.

Francis's case is extreme, but preciousness about one's diet isn't just limited to health and fitness issues. One study showed that despite the pile of evidence indicating the value of family meals, many parents forgo family meals because they are not always able to afford the more expensive organic foods they would like to be able to serve their families (Bowen, Elliott, and Brenton, 2014). This rather misses the point of family mealtime; the opportunity for communion and communication should be the star, not what's on the plate.

Although it is important to take care of our bodies, our bodies cannot save us. Focusing on our bodies alone—either the pleasure they feel through overindulgence or the sense of control we can gain from depriving ourselves—cannot even produce a sense of well-being if we ignore other, significant areas of concern in our lives. So what is the answer?

The Heavenly Virtue of Temperance: The Antidote to Gluttony

The heavenly virtue of temperance, the ability to pursue every good thing in a healthy way, is the only way to reclaim the balance we need in order to achieve the wholeness we crave. Where gluttony gives the illusion of well-being—either by making us full or by giving us a sense of false control—temperance helps us to achieve balance in every aspect of life: work, play, relationships, and health. It facilitates mindful living by helping us find that balance that allows care, openness, acceptance, and love to grow. Truly, the only way to satisfy the divine longing for well-being and defeat gluttony is to commit to doing the work on oneself and one's relationships that leads to an authentic experience of wholeness. Temperance, because it encourages us to achieve an ecology between our internal and external worlds, enables us to appear fit on the outside and to be whole throughout. To neglect the psychological, relational, and spiritual work that we need to do and focus only on the externals of diet programs and gym memberships is to become what Jesus called "whitewashed tombs" (Mt 23:7). That is, whitewashed tombs that look beautiful on the outside but inside are full of death and dry bones.

Temperance facilitates our call to divinization in two ways. First, it makes us stop and ask the question "What do I really need?" Instead of mindlessly consuming food or drink, or mindlessly pursuing physical solutions to every problem, temperance enables us to pause, reflect, and identify what parts of our lives are really out of balance so we can respond not just to the hunger for food but also to the hunger for meaning, purpose, healthy connection to God and others, and a peaceful spirit.

Psychologists refer to the ability to be aware of one's true needs as *mindfulness*. Christians might do well to think of mindfulness as temperance in action. By facilitating mindfulness, temperance helps us monitor small positive or negative shifts in each of the five major areas of well-being we discussed at the beginning of the chapter, and to make appropriate plans to adjust for any imbalance we might be experiencing. The exercise of this ability enhances our sense of healthy self-control (Teper and Inzlicht, 2013). The mindfulness cultivated by practicing temperance has been shown to have multiple, direct health benefits, from decreasing stress (Creswell, Pacillio, Lindsay, and Brown, 2014) and mediating the impact on physical health of depression and anxiety (Kurdyak, Newman, and Segal, 2014), to lowering blood pressure (Hughes, Fresco, Myerscough, et al., 2013) and enhancing health outcomes for patients suffering from coronary heart disease and diabetes (Keyworth, Knopp, Roughley, Dickens, et al., 2014) and even from cancer (Newswise, 2014). Not surprisingly, with all these positive health benefits, research has found that people who cultivate the healthy self-control that accompanies temperance live significantly longer than those who don't (Turiano, Chapman, Agrigroaei, et al., 2014). In fact, participants in the latter study who reported poorer degrees of temperance in their lives were three times more likely to die during the period of the study than those who exhibited higher degrees of temperance.

The second way that practicing temperance facilitates the call to divinization is by ensuring that every part of us is exposed to God's grace so that our personal, emotional, social, and spiritual selves can be developed to their fullest potential. Recall that nothing that is imperfect can enter into the full presence of God (Rv 21:27). Temperance facilitates our growth in perfection by putting us in touch with each part of ourselves that could benefit from some attention, and making sure that no single dimension of our well-being consumes all of our energy at the expense of every other part of ourselves.

In sum, temperance is a key ingredient for an abundant, healthier, happier, and longer life in this world and the next! It is the virtue that enables us not merely to survive in this world, but to thrive.

Satisfying Your Divine Longing
for Well-Being: An Exercise

PRAY

Lord Jesus Christ,

I give you every part of my life. I give you my health, my relationships, my work, my quest for meaning, and my pursuit of enjoyment. Teach me to live my life in balance that I might praise you and glorify you with the choices I make. Teach me to be temperate in all things, that I might allow your grace to develop every part of me to my fullest capacity so that one day I may be perfected through that grace and be made worthy to fulfill my destiny to partake in your divine nature. I ask this in the Name of Jesus Christ, Lord of every part of my life. Amen.

COAL: Fuel for Change

As you reflect on ways you can satisfy your divine longing for well-being, take a moment to consider how COAL can help fuel the changes you would like to make in your life.

CURIOSITY AND OPENNESS

Ask yourself: Where did I learn that food (or managing my relationship with food) was the primary means to fulfillment?

Who taught me this response?

What situations impressed this lesson on me?

> Do I want to continue to allow these experiences to rule my life?

Do not judge or edit yourself. Receive your answers in a spirit of openness and grace.

ACCEPTANCE

Say, "These are the experiences that have shaped my struggle to satisfy my divine longing for well-being. I accept my past even as I accept God's call to change and grow."

LOVE

Loving myself means working to become the person God wants me to be. I know that I can fulfill my deepest longing for well-being only by being temperate and tending to each part of my life so that I may live and grow in balance.

> What specific areas of my life do I feel drive my less healthy relationship with food (e.g., my physical, psychological, social, spiritual well-being or how I pursue pleasure)? What could I do to pay more attention to these areas of my life?
>
> What obstacles would I have to overcome to achieve this goal?
>
> What help, resources, or support might I need to overcome these obstacles?
>
> Say, "I will love myself and accept God's love for me by choosing this path of temperance over the temptation to gluttony."

Review these loving resolutions each morning. Imagine a time in the coming day when you might be tempted to gluttony. Imagine responding instead with temperance by identifying the real hunger and meeting it instead of overfocusing on your relationship with food. Ask for God's help to remember this more loving response in those times when you are feeling tempted to be overly concerned with eating or with managing your relationship to food.

Practicing Temperance: Action Items

IF YOU TEND TO OVEREAT

Before you eat, offer up a brief prayer: "Lord, fill me up. Remind me what I truly hunger for and help me to refrain from using food as a means of distracting myself from meeting my deepest needs."

Ask, "What am I eating for?" "Am I hungry?" If "no," then ask yourself, "How might my time be better spent?"

Give up your membership in the clean plate club. Practice leaving a little bit of each item on your plate. Or, if you are serving yourself, put the regular amount you would take on your spoon or fork and then, before putting it on your plate, put a little bit back in the pot or serving dish.

Eat more slowly. Put down your utensils between bites. Thoroughly chew all your food. Swallow and wait a second before picking up your utensil to take another bite. Remember what you learned in the chapter on wrath. Slowing yourself down improves your self-control.

Of course, fasting is an ancient and important practice. Skip a meal once in a while and donate the equivalent cost of the meal to a charity of your choice.

IF YOU TEND TO BE MORE PRECIOUS ABOUT YOUR FOOD CHOICES

Unless your diet has been restricted by a physician or certified nutritionist, realize that your food preferences are just that, preferences.

Realize that at mealtime, being good company is more important than guarding your food choices. Eat as close to what your company is eating as possible.

By all means, feel free to follow your food preferences at home. But unless your doctor or nutritionist has restricted your diet, when you are eating at the home of a friend or family member, eat what you are served without complaint.

At restaurants, as above, be conscious of your doctor's orders. But having chosen the most agreeable meal, eat it as it comes without requesting special attention or fuss to be made over you or your meal. Care more about the people serving you than about your food preferences.

The Divine Longing for Well-Being: A Promise

In the Gospels, Jesus was often called "Rabbi" or "teacher." Let God teach you to live your life in balance, to slowly heal from your tendency to use your relationship with food as the primary way you achieve comfort or control in your life (either in terms of how much you consume or how much you care about what you consume). By seeking to live a more temperate life, you will allow God to perfect every part of you and lead you to perfect union with him. You will discover the secret to thriving, that is, the secret to developing every aspect of yourself and practicing temperance to keep those aspects of your well-being working in harmonious, joyful balance.

Chapter Ten

Satisfying the Divine Longing for Communion

I do not ask on behalf of these alone, but for those
also who believe in Me through their word; that
they may all be one; even as You, Father, are in
Me and I in You, that they also may be in Us, so
that the world may believe that You sent Me. The
glory which You have given Me I have given to
them, that they may be one, just as We are one.

—John 17:20-21

Deep in our heart of hearts we ache for connection with others. We long to know and be known by another, to be cherished, to be able to give ourselves freely and to receive another with abandon. It is among our deepest desires for every part of ourselves to be loved—especially the unlovable parts. Even in the face of all the sickness and poverty that Blessed Teresa of Calcutta (Mother Teresa) witnessed, she observed, "The most terrible poverty is loneliness and the feeling of being unloved." This deep human ache for connection is the heart of our divine longing for communion.

The Divine Longing for Communion

Although the divine longing for communion can be described as a deep desire for connection, intimacy, and love, there is something essential we need to know about it. It is a call from the deepest heart of God to the deepest part of our hearts.

Of course, the word "communion" makes many of us think of the Eucharist, and rightly so. But Communion isn't just a proper noun; *it is a promise* from God. The Eucharist represents God's promise that the ache welling up from the depth of our being to be one with him and all of humankind *will be fulfilled.* Communion takes its name from the very longing it seeks to fulfill. The human person longs to belong to another and, ultimately, to the Divine other. We sense that we are complete only when we give ourselves totally to another and receive the other totally in return. On earth, the most common way to fulfill this longing for connection is marriage, but, of course, the most profound, loving marriage can only point to the depth of intimacy we can hope to achieve in the presence of God as part of the Communion of the Saints.

The Root of Our Longing for Communion

This desire for communion is not merely psychological; it is an integral part of what it means to be human on a biological and spiritual level as well. St. John Paul the Great taught in his theology of the body that as far as humans are concerned, there is no such thing as an individual. We are all persons who, by nature, exist in communion with other humans. In fact, our biology speaks to this need in dramatic ways.

The need for communion is such a deep, basic need that babies will develop a condition known as *failure to thrive,* in which they refuse food to the point of starving themselves to death if they are not touched, held, and loved enough. Psychiatrist John Bowlby's observations of parent-infant interactions and their significance for the social, psychological, and biological development of the person form the basis of what psychologists refer to as *attachment theory*. According to attachment theory, the patterns of how quickly, generously, and attentively our parents respond to our needs for food, comfort, and affection actually become encoded into our nervous system, determining how well developed the social brain (the structures of our brain responsible for empathy, self-control, response flexibility, moral reasoning, pro-social behavior, and a host of other skills that make us human) will ultimately become (Siegel, 2012; Cozolino, 2014). All of this speaks to the fact that as human beings, not only do we desire communion: we need communion to become fully human in the first place, and, ultimately, we need to restore communion with God and humankind to fulfill our destiny to become gods through God's grace.

Based on this basic biological need for communion, St. John Paul the Great wrote of what he called the "nuptial meaning of the body." Of course the word "nuptial" usually refers to a wedding, and this case is no different, except as St. John Paul the Great used the term to refer to the wedding that occurs upon the fulfillment of the *unitive way* of our spiritual journey—the Wedding Supper of the Lamb, where we will achieve oneness with God and the Communion of the Saints.

In his theology of the body, St. John Paul the Great argues that God created our bodies to need communion specifically so that our very human nature could orient us toward the heavenly communion for which we are destined. Recall God's words at the dawn of creation: "It is not good for the man to be alone" (Gn 2:18). Human beings use a vocabulary of words and gestures. *But creation itself is the Divine vocabulary.* God speaks and things come into being. In those words "It is not good for the man to be alone," God spoke a need for communion into our biology—our very genetic make-up—so that no matter how far away from him we wandered, there would always be some part of us that was undeniably pointing the way back to him. We could refuse to listen to God's call to communion, but we would never stop feeling the urge. It seems odd, but St. Augustine and cognitive neuroscience appear to be in agreement on the subject of our innate striving for union with God. While Augustine reminds us that the human heart is restless until it comes to rest in God, scientists who study the deepest functioning of the human brain "are becoming increasingly aware that a metaphysical outlook may be so deeply ingrained in human thought processes that it cannot be expunged" (Vittachi, 2014). At the beginning of time, we were created to live in communion, and even now, fallen as we are, the deepest parts of us point to our destiny: an eternity living in communion with God and the saints at the eternal wedding feast.

The Nuptial Meaning of the Body

But if humankind was *created* in a state of communion (i.e., Original Unity) and is likewise *destined* for communion with God and the saints through divinization, what about now? In the present, we experience the nuptial meaning of our bodies in the desire man and woman have for each other. Ephesians 5:32 reminds us that the communion between husband and wife is a sign of Christ's union with the whole church. Recall what I mentioned previously about the nuptial meaning of our bodies. St. John Paul the Great asserted that God created man and woman in such a way that they would desire to make a gift of themselves to each other (2006). He created their bodies so that they could give and receive each other freely, totally, faithfully, and fruitfully. Through the act of lovemaking, the two become one on every level. As I note in my book *Holy Sex!*, this oneness doesn't last only as long as the man and woman are engaged in sex (Popcak, 2007). Intercourse creates a lasting union between the husband and wife, not just on a spiritual level, but also on a physiological level, as the neurochemicals released during lovemaking wire the partners' brains to think of each other as if they were part of the same body. Because of this wiring, healthy interactions between husband and wife positively impact the physical well-being of both partners, and threats to the integrity of the relationship (arguments, separation, etc.) undermine the partners' health, causing the same pain centers of the brain to light up that turn on when a person suffers physical injury (Beckes, Coan, and Hasselmo, 2013).

The desire that man and woman have for each other is a sign of the longing God has in his heart to be one with us (see Eph 5:32). God, of course, is not sexual. He doesn't have a body. But he is nuptial in the sense that he longs for loving, creative union with us. He longs to give himself fully to us and to receive us fully in return. In the Easter Vigil prayer known as *The Exultet,* we sing that "heaven is wedded to earth" on the cross when Jesus Christ gave himself freely, totally, faithfully, and fruitfully to humankind in the ultimate act of selfless love.

Christians believe that when a man and woman give themselves to each other in marriage, they become an icon of that heavenly union. To put it in simpler terms, in marriage, the husband and wife become physical signs of the free, total, faithful, and fruitful love God has in his heart for each of them. When a husband and wife love each other this way, in every part of their relationship, including their sexual lives, they can experience a taste of the immense bounty of love God has in store for them in the heavenly communion that will supersede marriage. When Jesus says there is no marriage in heaven (Mk 12:25), he is not looking down his nose at marital love. Rather, he is pointing to the fact that in the Communion of the Saints we will experience the fulfillment of the nuptial union (though not a sexual union) with God and all of humankind, of which a man and woman can experience only a taste in marriage.

Of course, not all people will marry, but every human being's body—married or not—speaks to the nuptial nature of the human person. In other words, every person was created by God to freely give of themselves to others through loving acts of generous service. When we take up this invitation, we discover how striving for communion with others by service to others enables us to discover ourselves. In the words of the Second Vatican Council in *Gaudium et Spes*, "[Christ] implied a certain likeness between the union of the divine Persons, and the unity of God's sons in truth and charity. This likeness reveals that man, who is the only creature on earth which God willed for itself, cannot fully find himself except through a sincere gift of himself."

Lust: A Distortion of the Divine Longing for Communion

The deadly sin of lust represents a distortion of the divine longing for communion. Satan knows that the human longing for communion is so deeply ingrained in us that he cannot obliterate it, so he twists that ache in such a way that we come to believe that mere physical connection will satisfy the longing for communion.

It is staggering to observe the various ways our culture positively worships lust. According to some estimates, people spend $16 billion annually on pornography. And we don't sacrifice just our money to lust. We sacrifice time too. ABC News reported that pornography use costs employers $11 billion annually in lost productivity. You might think that after spending all that money and time, our lust would be slaked, but the truth is, we can never get enough of what we don't really want. And no one really wants lust.

Many people think that Christians—Catholics in particular—are opposed to lust because they hate sex. To the contrary, Catholics recognize the spiritual power of sex. As Pope Benedict XVI observed, a healthy sense of eros (that is, one united to godly love of another) allows the man and woman to "rise in ecstasy toward the divine" (2005). The Church teaches that marriage is not so much the sacrament of doing the dishes together as it is the sacrament of sexuality. Sacraments use physical "stuff" to convey God's grace. Baptism uses water as the sacramental stuff that effects the birth of new spiritual children of God. The Eucharist uses bread and wine as the sacramental stuff to make us God's very own flesh and blood. Marriage uses sex as the sacramental stuff for reorienting us to the

Original Unity between man, woman, and God, and sex is a physical sign of the passion with which God loves each one of us. Contrary to popular opinion, Christianity—and Catholic Christianity in particular—is anything but a sex-phobic religion.

Love Versus Use

So why *are* we so down on lust? Perhaps St. John Paul the Great said it best when he noted that the opposite of love is not hate but use. When we love someone, we work to help them become more of the person they already are, but when we use someone, we *thingify* them, we reduce them to a tool we can use. Authentic love, expressed through what I like to call "holy sex" (Popcak, 2007), is not only pleasurable but also affirming of our humanity. It helps us overcome shame and embrace healthy vulnerability, brings new life into the world, unites two people into one, and is a source of health and well-being. By contrast, lust, because it treats the self and the other as objects, undermines our humanity, causes shame and a fear of vulnerability, fears and even despises new life, alienates people first from themselves and then from others, and is the source of disease and death. The sin of lust has everything to do with treating a person as an object, but we were simply not designed for this.

When something is treated in a manner for which it was not designed, it breaks down. For instance, a toaster makes a terrible hammer and tends not to make much toast after you've tried to pound a nail into the wall with it. In a similar way, humans, who were designed for love, break down and have a harder time giving and receiving true love and experiencing communion when they have been used by others or have used themselves through lust. A California State University study published in the *Journal of Sex Research* found that people who engage in casual sex report a lower sense of well-being and higher rates of anxiety and depression than those who do not (Bersamin, Zamboanga, Schwartz, et al., 2014). Likewise, researchers at the University of Virginia found that couples who had multiple sexual partners before marriage reported significantly less marital satisfaction than those who had fewer partners or were virgins at the time of their wedding (Rhoades and Stanley, 2014).

St. Thomas Aquinas observed that death is the unnatural separation of body and soul. Lust is a deadly sin because, like death, it unnaturally separates the body from the soul in our relationships with others. Where the divine longing for communion prompts us to give as much of ourselves as is appropriate to a particular relationship so that we may be truly known by the other person, lust wants us to be stingy, giving only enough of ourselves that we can create the illusion of knowing and being known by another. Unfortunately, illusions never satisfy.

Counselors who treat the problem sexual behaviors caused by lust know that people who struggle with lust often feel frustrated in their attempts to create deep, intimate connection with other people. The more serious a person's struggle with lust, the more they tend to struggle with effectively communicating their needs and emotions, being competent at negotiation and problem-solving, and making themselves vulnerable, in healthy ways, to others. Only by addressing these underlying problems—problems that, not coincidentally, directly impact the person's ability to meet their divine longing for communion with others—

can individuals struggling with lust experience relief from their compulsions.

Tom has been married for ten years. He is a good husband to Maryann and a loving father to their three children. He is active in his parish and likes to help the pastor with various projects as he can. That is why Maryann was so devastated when she caught Tom masturbating in front of his laptop one night. She had gone to bed early but came down for a drink. She thought she would check in on Tom, who said he had some work to catch up on. That's when she found him in front of the computer.

Enraged, she made him show her his browsing history and the other sites he had visited. After arguing late into the night, Tom confessed that, like many men, he had been using pornography since he was a teenager. Although he always thought his desire for porn would stop once he was married, he found the urge actually got stronger. It had gotten to the point where he was masturbating more days than not. He didn't know why. He was ashamed. Tom told Maryann that he often confessed his struggle, and after confession he could abstain for several days, but the urge always came back with a vengeance. He tried to reassure Maryann that he didn't want to do it and that it wasn't her fault, but she was devastated.

At Maryann's insistence, Tom sought counseling. Tom says, "When I went for my first appointment, I spent most of the time talking about my long-term struggle with porn and all the things I'd tried to do to stop. About half an hour into my monologue, the therapist asked me whether I was able to be honest with Maryann about my feelings and needs. At first I thought he meant sexually, but he clarified that, yes, he meant that too, but primarily he was asking about my ability to communicate my feelings and needs in general.

"The question confused me at first, but the more I thought about it, the more I realized that I really did tend to clam up about things. I mean, I'll talk about what happened in the day and things like that, but when it comes to telling her—or anyone, really—what I need, I tend to just keep that stuff to myself.

"Growing up, we didn't talk much about feelings. I was raised to think that if you needed something, you didn't bother other people with it; you just handled it. My counselor helped me realize that while that attitude served me well in some ways, it kept me isolated and frustrated in other ways. He helped me see that what I thought was "being responsible" was actually keeping people from being there for me.

"He asked me to do two things that were tremendously helpful. First, he told me that if I felt tempted to watch porn or masturbate, I should remind myself that what I was really craving was some kind of connection with another person. In fact, he explained that that's why I usually felt depressed after I masturbated. I wanted connection, but I couldn't get it through porn. He suggested that instead of just going along with the urge to view pornography, I should think of some small act of service I could do for the people around me, or some way I could reach out for connection with others. He helped me come up with a list of things I could do at home or at the office too.

"The second thing he asked me to do was keep a log every day of how I was feeling, the high and low points of my day, and what I felt I might have needed to feel better or more in control of my life. We focused on control because, for me, that was a big driver of my use of porn. I'd have a bad day and feel out of control, and instead of thinking about what I could do to get things on track, I'd go online.

"It wasn't easy for me to talk about that kind of stuff in general, especially with Maryann. But even though she didn't always understand what I was talking about at first, I found that if I kept trying to talk through things, we'd get there eventually. It was weird, but I found that the more I could be open about my feelings and needs with Maryann, even when I didn't get that need met—whatever it was—I still had less temptation to give in to porn. I still have to keep practicing, but what I have learned in counseling has made a huge difference. The more I go out of my way to let people in, especially my wife, the easier it's getting for me to resist that urge to masturbate."

Tom discovered that he was keeping people at arm's length by not sharing his needs. His repressed desire for real connection drove him to seek at least the illusion of intimacy with his fantasy life and the Internet. There are many different ways we isolate ourselves and try to protect our hearts, and many of them tend to push us toward sexual acting out as a way of filling the gap that's left by our unfulfilled yet innate need for connection with others.

Many people think that only men lust, but that isn't true. Remember, broadly understood, lust is when you try to use another person, when you treat another person as an object that exists for your pleasure.

Annette has never had a difficult time finding a boyfriend. Besides being quite attractive, she has a bubbly and outgoing personality that draws other people to her, men in particular.

Annette was surprised to discover that she was guilty of using the men in her life. She was out with friends at a bar. As usual, she didn't bring any money with her. She didn't normally have to. There was always some guy who was willing to pay for a drink or an appetizer. But this one time, one of her friends— actually a guy she has a little crush on—criticized her when she asked if he would mind buying her a drink because she had "accidentally" left her wallet at home.

"He said he knew it wasn't an accident," Annette said. "That we've been out together plenty of times and it's always the same thing. He said he'd be happy to buy me a drink or even dinner if I wanted, but only if I promised to pay him back. He said that he didn't like how I used guys to make me feel good about myself. He thought I was a better person than that, and he didn't feel like being used or supporting my using him.

"I was furious. In fact, I made an excuse to go home shortly after. I mean, how dare he talk to me like that, right? But when I calmed down, I had to admit that he was mostly right. I like that guys are attracted to me, and I use it to get things from them, even when I have no intention of going out with them. It has been a long time since I've been in a real relationship with someone, and I haven't even missed it! It's funny. My girlfriends all talk about guys who make relationships all about them. They say that guys only want one thing, but I'm not sure I was really all that different. It wasn't about sex for me, but I was still using guys to stroke my ego. All I had to do was sit there and smile or flip my hair. It's silly, I know, but it works, and, after a while, it got to be enough for me. I didn't realize how little I was settling for."

Annette had to reckon with a hard truth—that she was using her sexuality in a self-serving way, that she had reduced herself to an object of desire and men to objects of gratification. In doing so, she had denied herself the connection to others that would have allowed her to be valued as a person and to treat the men in her life as real persons in return.

Of course, we don't just long for connection with other people. We long for ultimate connection with God. G. K. Chesterton once noted that "Every man who knocks on the door of a brothel is looking for God." He wasn't just being cheeky. Remember, the St. Augustine who joked, "God give me chastity, but not yet!" is the same St. Augustine who discovered that his heart would remain restless until it rested in God.

We can never draw close enough to another person to completely satisfy our longing for communion. No matter how close our relationships become, we still long to be closer. No person will ever be enough to make us feel totally complete. That's because our human relationships can only point to the one, ultimate relationship that will satisfy us ultimately—our relationship to God.

Even so, we can achieve the maximum fulfillment from all of our relationships, not just our romantic ones, by practicing the heavenly virtue of chastity.

The Heavenly Virtue of Chastity: The Antidote to Lust

"Chastity." What a horrible word. Or at least it's a word with a horrible reputation. Most people equate it with repression, but that is not the Catholic view at all. For the church, chastity represents the integration, not the denigration, of the person. The *Catechism of the Catholic Church* says:

> Chastity means the successful integration of sexuality within the person and thus the inner unity of man in his bodily and spiritual being. Sexuality, in which man's belonging to the bodily and biological world is expressed, becomes personal and truly human when it is integrated into the relationship of one person to another, in the complete and lifelong mutual gift of a man and a woman.
>
> The virtue of chastity therefore involves the integrity of the person and the integrality of the gift (*CCC,* no. 2337).

That's a mouthful. The short version is that the divine longing for communion prompts me to give as much of my whole self as is appropriate for a particular relationship so that I might be truly known by another person (and vice versa). Chastity is the virtue, the skill, that allows me to be fully loving at the right time and in the right way with the right person, and it orders all my relationships.

"But," you might ask, "how can chastity order *all* my relationships? All my relationships aren't sexual." Of course they are. While not every relationship is genital in the sense that not every relationship involves sexual intercourse, every relationship is sexual—in the broadest sense of the word—because every relationship involves both the sharing of oneself with another and generativity, that is, the creation of something that is bigger than oneself and potentially outlives the self (for example, friendship or, in marriage, a baby).

Anytime I share myself with another person, even in a platonic way, I am being sexual because the sharing of myself creates unity and generativity. If I perform some act of service for you, you feel more warmly toward me. That warmth generates a stronger friendship that will be bigger than the both of us and may even outlive us in the stories people tell about what great buddies we were.

Christians are called to be fully loving at all times. Chastity is the virtue that helps us determine what that means in a given situation. It helps us to order all our relationships. Chastity tells us how much or how little to share with our co-workers so that they can be our friends but not become our so-called "work spouse" (the person at work who is closer to us than our real spouse). Chastity is the virtue that prevents us from lying to others by saying "I am one with you forever!" with our bodies while saying "I enjoy hanging out with you once in a while" with our lives. Chastity actually challenges us to be more expressive in our sexuality when we are being physically intimate in the bedroom with our mate, but it also stops us from ravishing our mate in the grocery store, where the most fully loving thing to do is to get the milk while he or she gets the lettuce. Chastity is the virtue that helps us make sure we have both good and appropriate boundaries and, at the same time, are as generous with ourselves as we ought to be in more intimate relationships. Ultimately chastity enables us to be as fully known by another person—and to know the other in return—as is appropriate for the kind of relationship we have with that person and the context in which we find ourselves.

Chastity and Divinization

Chastity facilitates divinization by reminding us that we can meet only so much of our divine longing for communion through our relationships with others. As I mentioned earlier, no matter how close you get to the person you are closest to, there will always be a longing for more closeness still. This can lead some people to despair and others to become needy as they constantly demand more than the other would be capable of giving in any universe. Chastity prevents this by reminding us that our relationship with God is the ultimate communion, and that we can never be completely at peace unless or until we have achieved union with him. Our relationship with God doesn't take anything away from our earthly relationships. It simply helps us to have realistic expectations for what our earthly relationships can and can't do for us. With chastity, we make sure we save the God-shaped hole in our heart for God.

Satisfying Your Divine Longing for
Communion: An Exercise

PRAY

Lord Jesus Christ,

Help me to fulfill my longing for communion. My deep desire to know and be known by another, and, ultimately, to know and be known intimately by you, Lord. So often I am tempted to settle for the illusion of communion in my life. Show me the path to authentic connection. When I am tempted to lust, remind me what I am truly longing for, and give me the courage to reach out to make a genuine connection with those around me. Give me chastity that I might be capable of being fully loving and fully loved in every part of my life.

I ask this in the Name of Jesus Christ, Lord of every part of my life. Amen.

COAL: Fuel for Change

As you reflect on the insights in this chapter, take a moment to consider how COAL can help fuel the changes you would like to make to satisfy your divine longing for communion.

CURIOSITY AND OPENNESS

Ask yourself: Where did I learn to view other people as a means of satisfying my need for pleasure?

Who taught me this response?

What situations impressed this lesson on me?

> Do I want to continue to allow these experiences to rule my life?

Do not judge or edit yourself. Receive your answers in a spirit of openness and grace.

ACCEPTANCE

Say, "These are the experiences that have shaped my struggle to satisfy my divine longing for communion. I accept my past even as I accept God's call to change and grow."

LOVE

Loving myself means working to become the person God wants me to be. I know that I can fulfill my deepest longing for communion only by being chaste—that is, by learning how to be as fully loving as is appropriate based upon both the nature of my relationship and the circumstances I am in.

> What specific things do I believe tend to trigger my desire to use another person as an object of pleasure or satisfaction? What could I do to become more aware of these triggers? What could I do to neutralize these triggers?

> What obstacles would I have to overcome to achieve this goal?

> What help, resources, or support might I need to overcome these obstacles?

Say, "I will love myself and accept God's love for me by choosing this path of chastity over the temptation to treat others as a means to an end (i.e., lust)."

Review these loving resolutions each morning. Imagine a time in the coming day when you might be tempted to lust. Imagine responding instead with chastity by identifying the real source of your longing for communion and making a plan to meet it instead of indulging the temptation to lust. Ask for God's help to remember this more loving response in those times when you are feeling tempted to think of another person as the source of pleasure or personal satisfaction.

Practicing Chastity: Action Items

Remember that chastity is about pursuing healthy connection with all the people in your life. To that end, practice asking yourself the following question throughout the day: "What can I do right now that would be an appropriate way to make a connection with someone in my life?"

Ask: "Am I as generous in my relationships as I ought to be?" Choose one relationship where it would be appropriate to give a little more of yourself. What could you do to be more loving and create closer connection with this person?

Consider: Is there someone in your life who is closer to you than they should be? What boundaries would you need to set to make this relationship healthier?

The Divine Longing for Communion:
A Promise

Remember Jesus's prayer that all might be one with one an-other and in him. It is God's deepest desire to satisfy your longing for communion. If you have been tempted to lust in the past, I hope that you will be able to see that what you truly desire is heart-to-heart connection with God and the people in your life. Even if you aren't sure how to make that happen or don't believe it is possible, give this desire to God and ask him to teach you how to fulfill this longing for con-nection with others and with him.

When you stop settling for the illusion of connection, God will make room in your heart for real communion. He will fill you up to overflowing, and your joy will be full (Rom 15:13).

Chapter Eleven

Approaching Divinity:
The Ladder of Divine Love

Draw near to God in confidence, and you will
receive strength, enlightenment, and instruction.
—*St. John of the Cross,* Sayings of Light and Love, *no. 63*

The Spanish mystic St. John of the Cross compared the process of divinization to the ladder a lover leans against his beloved's window on the night of their elopement. He called this the "ladder of divine love."

Although climbing the ladder takes real effort, it isn't a task to be taken up grudgingly. We're not planning to paint the side of the house! We're eloping with our beloved! With each step we are falling more and more deeply in love with God, who is our beginning, middle, and end. With each step, we become a little more amazed by how wonderful our God is, and a little more astonished at the incredible works he is doing in our lives, often without our even realizing it. Falling in love with God is like falling in love with the man or woman of our dreams, only it's a million times better. There is nothing boring or dutiful about falling in love. It is a source of endless fascination, exploration, transformation, and joy. Our union with God, the completion of our divinization, is not merely some self-improvement project, a duty that demands to be met, or a job that needs to be completed. It is our joyful participation in the greatest love story ever told.

Climbing the Ladder of Divine Love

In the first stage of divinization—known as the *purgative way*—we begin to climb the ladder of divine love by learning to (as Augustine put it) "trample our vices underfoot."

Higher up the ladder—on the *illuminative way*—we climb more confidently, using the sturdier rungs made of the divine longings of the human heart. At this second stage, we no longer experience our desires as a distraction. Instead, we undergo a total reorientation of our desire, enabling us to single-mindedly focus on drawing closer to God and fulfilling his mission in our lives. As we respond more perfectly to each of our seven divine longings, we don't just draw closer to our true selves; we also draw closer to God. The increased sense of abundance, dignity, justice, peace, trust, well-being, and communion that we receive as gifts *from* God are really an experience of a deeper participation in the life *of* God as we climb the ladder of divine love.

Nearing the top of St. John of the Cross's ladder, we enter the *unitive way* and the final stages of our divine transformation. Finally, we are ready to fall into the arms of our betrothed, the God whom St. Catherine of Sienna called her "mad lover."

Stepping into the Divine Fire

Reaching the top of the ladder and climbing through the window, we find ourselves in a room that is completely dominated by an immense hearth with a roaring fire.

Suddenly, we have a sense that a voice is calling to us through the flame, telling us to draw closer, to step into the fire. With clarity beyond all doubt, we know that this is no ordinary fire, but still we're afraid. Do we trust this voice calling us forward? Do we dare attempt the impossible? As warm as we are standing outside the hearth, we know that there is so much more warmth within the fire. No matter how much light fills the room from the fire, it can't compare to the brightness contained within the fire itself. And now the fire itself is calling us to step into the flames. It is no longer enough to be warmed by the fire. We ache to be filled with it.

And so we step into the flames, and the fire of God's life begins to fill us up and set us ablaze. It is a fascinating, and joyful, and overwhelming experience all at once. Fearful of being consumed by the flames, we're terrified that we won't be consumed. Up to now, we've been afraid we would lose ourselves if we got too close to the fire. Now we're finding that the more we are consumed by the fire, the more "ourselves," the more authentic, we become. We enter completely into the numinous experience Rudolf Otto proclaimed to be *mysterium tremendum, et fascinans*—mysterious, terrifying, yet irresistibly fascinating.

As more of us is consumed, we become more and more anxious to be totally united with the fire. We see the work God is doing in us, and we yearn for that work to be completed. We feel the joyful agony of a million small children on a thousand Christmas Eves filled with desperate anticipation of the amazing gifts the morning will bring. The greatest pleasures this earth can give fail to compare to the joy we know is coming, and it can't come quickly enough. We are traveling through the agony and the ecstasy that attends the *dark night of the soul,* that time when one can do nothing but ache for that last moment of total surrender, where every dream of this world is merely a distraction, a pale shadow of the bright dawn that is soon to come, and in which we have been granted the privilege of participating.

Finally, we are a flame in the fire. Eternal, bright, and perfect, we are consumed by the flames, but rather than being destroyed by them, we are glorified in them. We remain uniquely and unrepeatably ourselves, but ever more so. We become one more bright way the fire reveals itself to the world and calls others to itself in an ever expanding cycle of light and warmth and beauty.

The flames I am describing, of course, are grace, God's very own divine life, which at first warms us, then sets us ablaze, and then consumes us, drawing us into his very own self. The farther we progress down the path of theosis, the more we become partakers in God's divine nature. The fire of his love no longer simply warms us or burns within us. It becomes us, or, perhaps more accurately, we become it, as we enter into the very heart of God's burning passion for us.

Receiving the Heart of God

God loves us so much! It sounds trite to say it in such simple words, but it is infinitely true! God's love is so deep, so powerful, so profound, it is often simply easier to passively ignore it than actively try to comprehend it.

By analogy, on a purely human level, I often feel frustrated in my efforts to communicate my love for my wife. I tell her. I try to show her in what small ways I can. But it never feels like enough to me. I sincerely believe that if she knew how much I really love her, she would start to glow with the passion that burns in my heart for her. Sometimes I will tell her that I wish I could take out my heart and put it into her so that she could feel everything I feel for her and see everything I see in her. But of course I can't do that.

But God can. And he does. That is what grace is, the very life of God in us. When God gives us his grace, it is like he is taking his heart—beating with love and passion and joy—out of his own chest and placing it in ours so that we can be filled with everything he feels for us and see all the wonders he sees when he looks at us through his eyes of love.

St. Margaret Mary Alacoque experienced visions of our Lord in which he held his heart in his hands, extending it to her as a sign of his love and passion. In those visions, she heard our Lord say, "Behold the heart that has so loved humankind." God loves you so much that he wants to place his Sacred Heart in your chest, that you could feel the constant beat of his love filling you up in the deepest parts of yourself.

The spiritual journey is not a guilt trip. It is not a trail of tears we walk for a cruel, heavenly master who demands either perfection or death. It is a honeymoon, where our heavenly Lover runs to meet us, to save us from ourselves, and to make us whole with his love so that we can live together in joy and passion for all eternity.

> Hark! The sound of my lover! Here he comes
> springing across the mountains,
> leaping across the hills.
> My lover is like a gazelle
> or a young stag.
> See! He is standing behind our wall,
> gazing through the windows,
> peering through the lattices.
> My lover speaks and says to me,

"Arise, my friend, my beautiful one,
and come!" (Sg 2:8-10)

Throughout this book we have explored the seven divine longings of your heart: the longings for abundance, dignity, justice, peace, trust, well-being, and communion. Each of these longings is really an invitation from God to join him at the altar of the eternal wedding feast. Through these longings, God gets down on one knee and holds out not a ring but his Sacred Heart. *He is proposing* to make you whole, and to show you how you can live in his love for all eternity. He is asking you if you would do him the honor of letting him fulfill your deepest desires so that you will never want for anything again, and so that you can discover how to love yourself the way he loves you.

The God of all creation, the King of Kings, Lord of Lords, God of Gods, the Savior of the world is humbling himself out of his love for you. He is down on one knee. He is holding his breath. *What will your answer be?*

Saying "I Do" to Our Divine Spouse

In my marriage counseling work, I remind couples that we never say "I do" once. Every day we have a million opportunities to say "I do." In fact, every day we also have a million opportunities to say "I don't" to our spouse. When I love my wife, when I treat her with dignity and respect, when I look for little ways to make her life easier and more pleasant, I say "I do." When I get too caught up in my own world to attend to her, when I fail to respect or honor her, when I fail to have her back, I say "I don't."

The spiritual walk is much the same. Each day, when we feel the ache that accompanies each of the seven divine longings at the center of our heart, we can either say "I do" or "I don't" to God's invitation to let him love us for all eternity. Each time we respond to our divine longings in a manner that is consistent with the heavenly virtues, we choose him. We say "I do." And each time we choose differently, we say "I don't," and a small part of us withers.

Learning to love, in general, isn't easy. Learning to love God is even more of a challenge. But learning to love is the only work that's really worth doing. Let him teach you. Give him all the deepest longings of your heart every moment of every day. Don't be ashamed. Don't be afraid. He loves every part of you, especially the parts that you are afraid are unlovable. He knows that behind the sins, and the brokenness, and the shame is something beautiful, *something divine*, and he has sacrificed everything to show you how beautiful you are, and how much more beautiful you can become if you will just place his heart next to yours.

Receive his love. Say "yes." And live!

Throughout this book, you have discovered that God has great plans for your life, perhaps even greater plans than you dared to believe were even possible.

Although your life contains great promise, fulfilling that promise can be a challenge. We often encounter many obstacles on the way. If you are struggling to carry out the ideas in this book, or are having a hard time finding God's peace, joy, and love in any part of your life or relationships, I would like to invite you to contact the Pastoral Solutions Institute to learn more about our Catholic tele-counseling practice.

Through the Pastoral Solutions Institute you can discover faith-filled and effective solutions to life's difficult challenges. We will help you apply the timeless wisdom of our Catholic faith and contemporary psychological insights to help you become everything God intends for you to be.

To learn more about the services we provide or to make an appointment to speak with a counselor, please call 740-266-6461 or visit us online at www.CatholicCounselors.com.

It is my deepest wish that God will bless you abundantly. May you delight in him, and may he teach you to satisfy all the desires of your heart according to his perfect will in Christ Jesus.

Yours in Christ,
Dr. Gregory Popcak, Pastoral Solutions Institute

Acknowledgments

What an honor it is to be able to write and publish on topics that are so close to my heart. When one is given such an honor, thanks are in order. The following represents my feeble attempt to fill that order as completely as possible.

First, I would like to thank my readers, of both my previous works and this most recent one. Without your continued interest, this effort would not be possible. I am incredibly touched that you have found something of value in my work, and I am grateful for your support over the years. I hope what you have read here will justify a long and continuing relationship.

Of course, heartfelt thanks are due to the people who made this book possible. First, to Michael Aquilina, who has always been a hero and mentor. Thank you for both your input that led to my proposing this title and for your kind words behind the scenes. An abundance of thanks, of course, goes to my editor, Gary Jansen. First, for your initial interest in the idea, then for not completely freaking out (at least not on me) when I originally turned in a manuscript that was nearly twice as long as it was supposed to be, and finally, for shepherding the book into its present, much less unwieldy and—hopefully—much more enjoyable form. Of course, I also owe a great debt to Maggie Carr, my intrepid copy editor, who braved the jungle of words I sent and tamed it so that others would be able to venture forth without getting lost.

I would also like to thank my chorus of readers and critics who helped me shape and develop my ideas. Thank you, Dr. Kevin Miller, for your invaluable feedback on the first several chapters, especially. If I somehow managed to not say anything heretical in the first one hundred pages or so, it is almost entirely his doing—whether or not he would ever be willing to admit it publicly. Thank you, Dave McClow, my colleague at the Pastoral Solutions Institute, for your interest and your willingness to assist with the research going into this book. The quotes and supporting resources you found were of inestimable help. A thousand blessings on your house! Thanks as well to Jacob Popcak, my son, best friend, and most helpful critic. This project would not have been as successful without your critical feedback about both the tone and content. Not only did you offer such terrific and insightful comments, but the book trailer you shot and edited was remarkable. I couldn't be prouder to be your dad. Many thanks also go to my wife, Lisa. Your input was so important and your unfailing support—especially through those grumbling, miserable few weeks when I had to find a way to cut the manuscript in half—will no doubt put you on the fast track to divinization. To be sure, I am not fit to tie your sandals, but thanks for having me all the same. Thanks as well to my beautiful daughters, Rachael and Liliana, who helped remind me what was most important and whose love keeps me going every day. Finally, I thank my mom and dad (may Perpetual Light shine upon him). You showed me how to love God up close and personal and taught me to take my first steps down this road. All of this is totally your fault, and there's nothing you can do about it now. So there.

REFERENCES

Arintero, J. 1979. *Mystical Evolution in the Development and Vitality of the Church.* Charlotte, NC: Tan Books.

Baram, T. 2008. "Short-term Stress Can Affect Learning and Memory." *Today at UCI. Science Daily.* Retrieved October 1, 2014, at http://archive.today.uci.edu/news/release_detail .asp?key=1743.

Barron, R. 2007. *Seven Deadly Sins, Seven Lively Virtues.* Skokie, IL: Word on Fire.

Beckes, L., J. Coan, and K. Hasselmo. 2013. "Familiarity Promotes the Blurring of Self and Other in the Neural Representation of Threat." *Social Cognitive and Affective Neuroscience* 8(6).

Bersamin, M. M., B. L. Zamboanga, S. J. Schwartz, et al. 2014. "Risky Business: Is There an Association Between Casual Sex and Mental Health Among Emerging Adults?" *Journal of Sex Research* 5(1):43–51.

Boniwell, I. 2012. *Positive Psychology in a Nutshell: The Science of Happiness.* UK: Open University Press.

Boston Catholic.org. n.d. Archdiocese of Boston. *Being Catholic. Quotes by Saints.* Retrieved December 22, 2014, at http://www.bostoncatholic.org/Being-Catholic/Content .aspx ?id=11480.

Bowen, S., S. Elliott, and J. Brenton. 2014. "The Joy of Cooking?" *Contexts* 13(3).

Carter, N. 2014. *We Are Not Broken. Godless in Dixie*. Patheos Atheist Channel. October 31. Retrieved November 14, 2014, from http://www.patheos.com/blogs/godlessindixie/2014/10/31/not-broken/.

Clores, S. (Ed.). 2002. *The Wisdom of the Saints*. New York: Citadel.

Cozolino, L. 2014. *The Neuroscience of Human Relationships: Attachment and the Developing Social Brain*. New York: W. W. Norton.

Creswell, J. D., L. E. Pacilio, E. K. Lindsay, and K. W. Brown. 2014. "Brief Mindfulness Meditation Training Alters Psychological and Neuroendocrine Responses to Social Evaluative Stress." *Psychoneuroendocrinology* 44: 1–12.

Denson, T., C. DeWall, and J. Finkel. 2012. "Self-control and Aggression." *Current Directions in Psychological Science* 21(1).

Dunn, E., L. Aknin, and M. Norton. 2014. "Pro-social Spending and Happiness: Using Money to Benefit Others Pays Off." *Current Directions in Psychological Science* 23(1):41–47.

Dunn, E. W., C. Ashton-James, M. D. Hanson, and L. B. Aknin, 2010. On the Costs of Self-interested Economic Behavior: How Does Stinginess Get Under the Skin? *Journal of Health Psychology* 15(4):627–633.

Feeney, B. C., and N. L. Collins. 2014. "A New Look at Social Support: A Theoretical Perspective on Thriving Through Relationships." *Personality and Social Psychology Review* 18(3).

Geliebter, A., and A. Aversa. 2003. "Emotional Eating in Overweight, Normal Weight and Underweight Individuals." *Eating Behavior* 3(4):341–347.

Harbaugh, W. T., U. Mayr, and D. R. Burghart, 2007. Neural Responses to Taxation and Voluntary Giving Reveal Motives for Charitable Donations. *Science* 316(5831):1622–1625.

Huffington Post. 2010. "Jillian Michaels: I Won't Ruin My Body with Pregnancy." Retrieved September 5, 2014, at http://www.huffingtonpost.com/2010/04/22/jillian-michaels-i-wont-r_n_548256.html.

Hughes, J., D. Fresco, R. Myerscough, et al. 2013. "Randomized Controlled Trial of Mindfulness-based Stress Reduction for Prehypertension." *Psychosomatic Medicine* 75(8).

Keyworth, C., J. Knopp, K. Roughley, C. Dickens, et al. 2014. "A Mixed-Methods Pilot Study of the Acceptability and Effectiveness of a Brief Meditation and Mindfulness Intervention for People with Diabetes and Coronary Heart Disease." *Behavioral Medicine* 40(2).

Kratina, K. n.d. "Orthorexia Nervosa." *National Eating Disorders Association.* Retrieved September 5, 2014, at https://www.nationaleatingdisorders.org/orthorexia-nervosa.

Kreeft, P. 1988. "Comparative Religions: Christianity and the New Paganism." *Fundamentals of the Faith: Essays in Christian Apologetics.* San Francisco: Ignatius Press.

Kurdyak, P., A. Newman, and Z. Segal. 2014. "Impact of Mindfulness-based Cognitive Therapy on Health Care Utilization: A Population-based Controlled Comparison." *Journal of Psychosomatic Research* 77(2).

Layous, K., J. Chancellor, S. Lyubomirsky, et al. 2011. "Delivering Happiness: Translating Positive Psychology Intervention Research for Treating Major and Minor Depressive Disorders." *Journal of Alternative and Complementary Medicine* 17(8).

Lewis, C. S. 1952. *Mere Christianity.* New York: Macmillan.

Marquardt, K. 2000. "Luther and Theosis." *Concordia Theological Quarterly* 64(3).

Meconi, D. 2014. *Pope John XXIII, 1958–1963: A Brief Biography. Homiletic and Pastoral Review.* http://www.hprweb

.com/2014/04/pope-john-xxiii-1958-1963-a-brief-biography/.

Newswise. 2014. "Mindfulness-based Meditation Helps Teenagers with Cancer." March 5. Retrieved September 5, 2014, from http://www.newswise.com/articles/mindfulness -based-meditation-helps-teenagers-with-cancer.

Pargament, K. 2011. *Spiritually Integrated Psychotherapy: Understanding and Addressing the Sacred.* New York: Guilford Press.

Pentin, E. 2014. "Pope Francis Top 10 List for Happiness." *National Catholic Register*, July 29. Retrieved July 29, 2014, at http://www.ncregister.com/daily-news/pope-francis-top -10-list-for-happiness/.

Popcak, G. 2007. *Holy Sex! The Catholic Guide to Toe-Curling, Mind-Blowing, Infallible Loving.* New York: Crossroad.

Pope Benedict XVI. 2005. *Deus Caritas Est.* Retrieved September 10, 2014, at http://www.vatican.va/holy_father/benedict _xvi/encyclicals/documents/hf_ben-xvi_enc_20051225 _deus-caritas-est_en.html.

————. 2012. General Audience, November 7. Retrieved July 14, 2014, at http://www.vatican.va/holy_father/benedict_ xvi/audiences/2012/documents/hf_ben-xvi_aud_20121107_ en.html.

Pope Francis. 2013. *Evangelium Gaudii.* Retrieved July 7, 2014, at www.Vatican.va.

Pope John Paul II. 2002. Opening Address at the 17th World Youth Day. Toronto. Retrieved July 28, 2014, at http:// www.vatican.va/holy_father/john_paul_ii/speeches/2002/ july/documents/hf_jp-ii_spe_20020725_wyd-address -youth_en.html.

————. 2006. *Man and Woman He Created Them: A Theology of the Body.* Trans. Michael Waldstein. Boston: Pauline Books and Media.

Pope Paul VI. 1967. *Populorum Progressio*. Vatican.va.

Rhoades, G., and S. Stanley. 2014. "Before 'I do': What Do Premarital Experiences Have to Do with Marital Quality Among Today's Young Adults?" National Marriage Project, University of Virginia.

Ryan, R., and E. Deci. 2001. "On Happiness and Human Potentials: A Review of Research on Hedonic and Eudaimonic Well-being." *Annual Review of Psychology* 52(1).

Seligman, M. 2002. *Authentic Happiness: Using the New Positive Psychology to Realize Your Potential for Lasting Fulfillment*. New York: Atria Books.

Shea, M. 2001. *Catholics and the Cult of Fun*. Mark-Shea.com.

Siegel, D. 2007. *The Mindful Brain. Reflection and Attunement in the Cultivation of Well-being*. New York: W. W. Norton.

———. 2012. *The Pocket Guide to Interpersonal Neurobiology: An Integrative Handbook of the Mind*. New York: W. W. Norton.

Spiegel Online International. 2006. "Pope Gives Interview: Benedict Says Catholicism No 'Collection of Prohibitions.'" Retrieved September 1, 2014, at http://www.spiegel.de/international/pope-gives-interview-benedict-says-catholicism-no-collection-of-prohibitions-a-431617.html.

Teichart, T., V. Ferrera, and J. Grinband. 2014. "Humans Optimize Decision-making by Delaying Decision Onset." *Plos One* 9(3), March 5. Retrieved September 4, 2014, at http://www.plosone.org/article/info%3 Adoi%2F10.1371%2F jour nal.pone.0089638.

Teper, R., and M. Inzlicht. 2013. "Mindful Acceptance Dampens Neuroaffective Reactions to External and Rewarding Performance Feedback." *Emotion* 14(1).

Thigpen, P. 2001. *The Saints' Guide to Making Peace with God, Yourself, and Others*. Ann Arbor, MI: Charis.

Turiano, N., B. Chapman, S. Agrigoroaei, et al. 2014. "Perceived Control Reduces Mortality Risk at Low, Not High, Education Levels." *Health Psychology* 33(8).

Vittachi, N. 2014. "Scientists Discover That Atheists Might Not Exist, and That's Not a Joke." *Science 2.0 Join the Revolution*. Retrieved September, 6, 2014, at http://www.science20.com/writer_on_the_edge/blog/scientists_discover_that_atheists_might_not_exist_and_thats_not_a_joke-139982.

Wedgeworth, S. 2011. "Reforming Deification." *Credenda Agenda: A Religiously and Philosophically Trinitarian Cultural Journal*. Retrieved April 18, 2014, at http://www.credenda.org/index.php/Theology/reforming-deification.html.

West, Christopher. 2012. *Fill These Hearts: God, Sex, and the Universal Longing*. New York: Image Books.

Wheeler, Mark. 2013. "Be Happy: Your Genes May Thank You for It." *UCLA Newsroom*. Retrieved August, 8, 2014, from http://newsroom.ucla.edu/releases/don-t-worry-be-happy-247644.

Wiseman, J. 2001. "The Body in Spiritual Practice: A New Asceticism." *Spiritual Life: A Journal of Contemporary Spirituality* 47(4).

Wooden, C. 2013. "Marriage Isn't Easy, but It's Beautiful, Pope Says." *Catholic News Service*. Retrieved August 12, 2014, at http://www.catholicnews.com/data/stories/cns/1304506.htm.

Zeller, B. 2014. "Ultimate Reality and Divine Beings." *Patheos Religion Library: New Age*. Retrieved May 24, 2014, at http://www.patheos.com/Library/New-Age/Beliefs/Ultimate-Reality-and-Divine-Beings.html.

Zenit. 2012. "Benedict XVI: God Wants Us to Be Happy Always." Retrieved July 28, 2014, at http://www.zenit.org/en/articles/benedict-xvi-god-wants-us-to-be-happy-always.

Additional Works Consulted

Bouyer, L. 2002. *The Christian Mystery: From Pagan Myth to Christian Mysticism.* London, UK: T & T Clark International.

Coe, J. 2000. "Musings on the Dark Night of the Soul: Insights from St. John of the Cross on a Developmental Spirituality." *Journal of Psychology and Theology* 28(4).

Groeschel, B. 1984. *Spiritual Passages: The Psychology of Spiritual Development.* New York: Crossroad.

Jacobs, J. 2009. "An Eastern Orthodox Conception of Theosis and Human Nature." *Faith and Philosophy* 26(5):615–627.

Keating, D. 2007. *Deification and Grace.* Washington, DC.: Sapientia Press.

Lehninger, P. D. 1999. "Luther and Theosis: Deification in the Theology of Martin Luther." PhD diss., Marquette University. *Dissertations (1962–2010).* Access via Proquest Digital Dissertations. Paper AAI9929163.

Louth, A. 2007. "The Place of Theosis in Orthodox Theology." In *Partakers of the Divine Nature: The History and Development of Deification in the Christian Tradition.* Ed. M. Christensen and J. Wittung. Grand Rapids, MI.: Baker Academic Press, pp. 32–44.

Ratzinger, J. 1986. *Behold the Pierced One.* San Francisco: Ignatius Press.

Ware, B. K. 2002. *The Orthodox Way.* Crestwood, NY: St. Vladimir's Seminary Press.